MARTHA ROSE SHULMAN

SPIRALIZE
this!

MARTHA ROSE SHULMAN

SPIRALIZE
this!

75 FRESH AND
IRRESISTIBLE
RECIPES FOR
YOUR SPIRALIZER

HOUGHTON MIFFLIN HARCOURT
BOSTON · NEW YORK · 2016

Copyright © 2016 by Martha Rose Shulman

For information about permission to reproduce selections from this book, write to trade.permissions@hmhco.com or to Permissions, Houghton Mifflin Harcourt Publishing Company, 3 Park Avenue, 19th Floor, New York, New York 10016.

www.hmhco.com

Library of Congress Cataloging-in-Publication Data is available.

ISBN 978-0-544-91367-7 (hbk)

ISBN 978-0-544-91368-4 (ebk)

Book design by Waterbury Publications, Inc.

Printed in China

TOP 10 9 8 7 6 5 4 3 2 1

To my sister, Melodie

CONTENTS

INTRODUCTION

"Now I get it!" said my sister, Melodie. "It's not that I don't like cooking; it's chopping I don't like!"

My sister, who has celiac disease and has not eaten gluten for years, was staying with me in Los Angeles, recovering from a fractured tibia that she suffered in a cycling accident. I was madly testing recipes for this book, and she was my willing eater. One beautiful and delicious dish followed another, and she was hooked—as was I—on this simple kitchen tool.

The spiralizer is much more than a gadget for turning vegetables into strands that can stand in for noodles in pasta dishes, a boon for those who love pasta but have a problem with wheat or carbs. It's a great prep tool for all sorts of vegetables—onions to potatoes, winter squash, zucchini—and far from limited to transforming them into pasta. Pass an onion through the fine blade and you'll get the thinnest slices possible in less than a minute, with no tears! When I was testing recipes, I diced and sliced innumerable potatoes, beets, zucchini, and peppers for frittatas and gratins, stir-fries and tacos, kugels and fajitas in no time. And it was fun. The tool is like a simplified version of a mandoline, but you don't risk cutting off the tip of your finger when you use it.

When I was working on this book, I lost weight. I didn't need to or mean to lose weight, but I was eating a very satisfying diet with the calories coming mainly from vegetables. If weight loss is a goal, start cooking your way

through the recipes in this book, and you will find yourself on a healthy diet without even being aware of it. There is nothing ascetic or restrictive about the recipes. But the fact that they are produce-centric—even those recipes that include eggs, dairy, cheese, and meat—means their calorie loads and glycemic indexes are low.

I didn't need to be eating more produce, but the spiralizer inspired me to create meals that had vegetables at their core. Every time I went to the market, I'd look at produce with a new eye. "Oh, I bet that would be fun to spiralize," I'd say as I grabbed items that I'd never paid much attention to before. And with that I'd come home with a bag full of kohlrabi that would end up as a delicious, creamy slaw that got wrapped into my chicken taco (page 133), or with celeriac or rutabaga that I transformed into noodles and tossed with kale, leeks, Gruyère, and Parmesan (page 115). When I looked at colorful watermelon radishes at the farmers market, I saw them as wide pink spiraled strands garnishing a zucchini noodle salad (page 26). Golden beets, sliced thin on the blade of my spiralizer, would stand in for lasagna noodles in a luxurious layered casserole (page 108).

It has always been my firm belief that the key to healthy eating begins with preparing your own meals. That is how you take control of what you eat. If, like my sister, you find kitchen prep work tedious, the spiralizer will help you enjoy cooking a little more. Not only does prep go quickly, but the cooking time for spiralized vegetable pasta strands is short—only 1½ minutes, 2 at most. This collection will inspire you to get into the kitchen and cook.

ABOUT THE RECIPES

The spiralizer has been associated with cooks who wish to eliminate grains and animal proteins from their diet. But these recipes are designed for a broader spectrum of eaters and cooks. I am neither vegan nor gluten-free, paleo nor strictly vegetarian (though the focus of my cooking is often meatless). I am a cook who has always had a healthy focus, and to me that means a dedication to a balanced diet with produce at its core.

The recipes in this book put produce front and center. Some of them are vegan, most are gluten-free, and many are suitable for those who follow a paleo diet. The dishes are meant to be appealing—even irresistible—for people who do not, as well as for people who do, eliminate certain food groups from their diet. For those who don't eliminate animal protein, there are plenty of wonderful dishes with eggs and cheese, as well as a few meat and fish recipes. There are also some sugary desserts. They belong here because the spiralizer makes them so much fun to prepare, and the results are gorgeous and delicious. The repertoire you will come away with is light and healthy. It will bring vegetables into your life and into the lives of your family and friends in ways you may have never imagined.

BASICS

There are two types of spiralizers on the market: smaller hand spiralizers and larger freestanding models. I find hand spiralizers more difficult to use than the freestanding models. Their one advantage is that they work a little better for thinner vegetables like carrots and broccoli stems, which are too thin to go through the freestanding models. Because spiralizers are not very expensive, I recommend having both.

Some hand models have a single blade and others have two—one for very fine shredding and one a little thicker. The standing spiralizers have an additional slicing blade, and some models have more than two sizes for shredding. My spiralizer came with three blades: the fine shredder blade, the coarse chipper blade, and the slicer blade. The slicer blade makes beautifully uniform, very thin slices, as well as flat, wide spiralized noodles that can stand in for pappardelle. Models with an additional blade have an angel hair blade.

HOW IT WORKS

The standing models affix to your work surface on suction cups. Place a sheet pan or a wide shallow bowl at the end to catch the spiralized vegetables, unless you use a spiralizer that comes with a catching vessel.

Affix the center of the vegetable or fruit on one end to the circular hold in the center of the blade (which also acts as a coring blade), and the other end to the pronged clamp. As you turn the crank, the item moves against the blades as the center moves through the hole (sort of like a pencil in a pencil sharpener), and long, curly strands or slices fall into the bowl or sheet pan. Once the vegetable or fruit has gone through as far as it will go, you're left with a mushroom-shape solid bit consisting of the middle that moved through the tube and the end affixed to the holder. You can use this for another purpose or cut it by hand.

An irregular shape piece of produce, like a curved zucchini or summer squash, will not move in a straight line through the spiralizer, and you will not get strands but rather curved C-shape pieces. This can be frustrating if your aim is long noodles. When you see this happening, stop spiralizing, pull the vegetable off the spiralizer, cut away the bit that went through the tube, and reposition the vegetable so it is centered. If you do get lots of C-shape pieces, just use them as you would shorter pasta shapes like fusilli. Or use them in other dishes like gratins and salads.

WHAT WORKS

- **Produce that is firm,** at least 1½ inches long, and at least 1½ inches in diameter. This eliminates most precut baby carrots, but full carrots are often wide enough at one end. I find it easiest to use a hand-held spiralizer for carrots and broccoli stems, because the pronged holder on the crank spiralizers can't get a good grasp on the narrow ends; they won't turn properly against the blade. I use my hand, rather than the prolonged handle, to turn the vegetables.

WHAT DOESN'T WORK

• **Produce that is soft or juicy.** It will give and fall apart or squish as you push it against the blade. This rules out juicy fruits and vegetables like tomatoes, citrus, pineapples, and mangos (which are also impossible to spiralize because they have a large seed in the middle), and soft fruits and vegetables like bananas, eggplants, avocados, and melons. Eggplant might appear firm, but the flesh has a spongy texture that will not stay intact when turned on the spiralizer; it will tear. Pears work if they are firm, even if they are on the juicy side.

• **Produce with lots of seeds or one big seed in the middle.** This rules out tree fruits and the bulbous ends of butternut squash, but the necks will work fine. It's another reason eggplant doesn't work well. The exception to this rule is thick-fleshed bell peppers. I use the spiralizer for peppers often, but I only spiralize a little more than halfway up the vegetable, until the blade reaches the seed pod. See the recipes for instructions.

• **Produce that is narrow,** like thin carrots and celery.

• **Produce that is irregular,** like cauliflower and broccoli florets. It's difficult to secure and will fall apart.

Here are the vegetables and fruits that work well. I have used most of them in the recipes in this book:

Apples	Parsnips
Asian pears	Pears
Beets	Peppers
Broccoli stems	Potatoes
Carrots (only fat ones)	Radishes
Celeriac	Rutabaga
Chayote	Sweet potatoes
Cucumbers	Turnips
Daikon radish	Watermelon radishes
Jicama	Winter squash
Kohlrabi	Zucchini and other
Onions	summer squash

Some cooks like to use the spiralizer for cabbage; they like the evenness of the shred. I find cabbage easier to shred by hand, but give it a try and see what you think.

Shredder blade half moons

Shredder blade noodles

Shredder blade rings

Slicer blade half moons

Slicer blade ribbons

Slicer blade slices

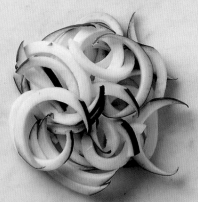

Chipper blade half moons

Chipper blade noodles

Chipper blade rings

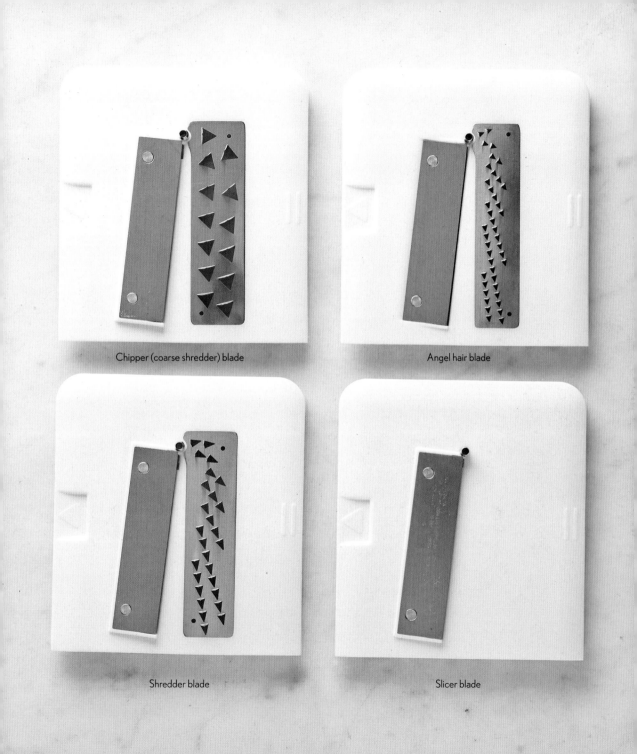

Chipper (coarse shredder) blade

Angel hair blade

Shredder blade

Slicer blade

PREPARING VEGETABLES FOR THE SPIRALIZER

- Trim the ends off so that each end is flat. Take care to cut straight across the ends so the produce will pass evenly through the spiralizer.

- Peel the vegetables (if they are to be peeled) before spiralizing. Some vegetables, like kohlrabi, winter squash, and celeriac, have a fibrous layer underneath the skin. Double peel these vegetables. Otherwise some of the strands will be tough and fibrous.

- Cut long vegetables into pieces no bigger than 3 to 4 inches long. This makes hard, heavy vegetables like winter squash easier to attach and manipulate, and it will also prevent uneven spiralizing if the vegetable has curves, as is often the case with zucchini and other summer squash. My one reservation about this is that you lose more of the vegetable, as there is always about ½ inch at the end that won't go through the spiralizer. Smaller pieces also yield shorter strands. However, I find it easy to cut long strands into manageable lengths using scissors.

- Even if you are using the spiralized vegetables for pasta dishes, the strands can be very long. I take up handfuls of the strands and snip with scissors for manageable lengths. For shorter lengths called for in other recipes, place spiralized produce in a bowl, point the scissors straight down into the bowl, and snip away.

- To obtain ring-shape or curved pieces rather than long strands, or flat slices, cut a ½-inch incision down the length of the vegetable. For C-shaped curves, cut the incision down two sides. Wide round vegetables will usually break into individual rounds as you cut them.

PREPARING APPLES, PEARS, AND ASIAN PEARS FOR THE SPIRALIZER

Peel the fruit, twist the stem to remove it, and cut the stem end flat if necessary so it will sit on the pronged holder. Insert the core (bottom) end into the corer blade. For softer pears, do not press hard when you spiralize or the fruit may fall apart. Because the core of most apples and pears is a little wider than the center core blade, it is difficult to avoid getting a few seeds or bits of seeds in with your spiralized fruit—just pick these bits out before you proceed with the recipe.

YIELDS

I find that no matter what vegetable I spiralize, yields are consistently uniform. A half pound of produce yields 2 cups of spiralized noodles. The volume reduces considerably when these vegetables are cooked, whether in boiling water, in a frying pan, or in the oven. For pasta, I calculate a half pound or 2 cups spiralized vegetable per serving; zucchini and summer squash lose more volume due to their water content, so you may want to calculate 10 ounces per person for those vegetables. If you are not using the vegetables as a pasta substitute, (for example, they are an ingredient in a frittata or a salad) you will often be instructed to cut the strands into approximately 2-inch lengths. Once cut, the volume will be smaller.

WORKING WITH WATERY VEGETABLES

Cucumbers and summer squash are watery. In the recipes you will be instructed to salt cucumbers and let them drain in a colander before using them in salads (they aren't cooked or used in pasta dishes in this collection). To dry them further, drain then purge on paper towels or dish towels.

I don't use watery sauces with summer squash pasta because zucchini and other summer squash release water after cooking. In fact, the squash provides welcome moisture for the pasta dish, and if you use enough salt in your cooking water, this liquid will be tasty. When I make a regular pasta-and-vegetable dish, I always use some of the pasta cooking water to moisten the mix (the starch in the water also contributes texture and helps bind the sauce I'm using with the noodles). With squash pasta this isn't necessary, as the squash continues to release water into the dish once it's tossed with the vegetables and olive oil. Because the water released by the squash will not be starchy, it's important to add a little olive oil, which contributes texture as well as flavor.

I cook the squash noodles very briefly in salted boiling water—1½ minutes maximum—and remove from the water with tongs or a skimmer and toss immediately with the accompaniment, which is usually a mix of vegetables, herbs, olive oil, and a bit of Parmesan and/or ricotta. If you serve the dish right away, the noodles won't have time to dilute the accompanying vegetables and release too big a pool of liquid. There will be some juice left in the bowl after you've tossed and served the zucchini noodles, but this never bothers me. Other noodles, like celeriac, rutabaga, and beets, do not become too watery.

VEGETABLE NOODLES THAT FALL APART

Winter squash and sweet potato noodles will fall apart in boiling water. Instead they can be tossed with olive oil and roasted in a 375-degree oven. See recipes for specific instructions.

PRODUCE THAT DISCOLORS

Once spiralized, white potatoes, kohlrabi, apples, and pears will oxidize quickly and discolor. Do not spiralize ahead of making the recipes, or in the case of fruit, toss with lemon juice.

PRODUCE THAT FALLS APART

Certain types of produce—jicama, Asian pears—have a crunchy, moist texture, and if they are very bulbous, the coils tend to break apart when I turn them in the spiralizer. I am not using these items as pasta substitutes, so I don't mind it when the coils break up. Don't be dismayed if this happens; you'll still be able to use the broken-up pieces in the recipes.

STORING SPIRALIZED PRODUCE

Spiralized produce, with the exception of the foods that oxidize, keeps well in the refrigerator. Store in resealable freezer bags or covered containers for up to 2 days. Cooked spiralized produce will keep for a day or two, but the watery vegetables like zucchini and cucumber continue to release water. It's best to store zucchini uncooked.

CLEANING AND SAFETY

Spiralizers are much safer to use than mandolines because the vegetables are held in place with an arm and turned using a crank. However, I have found that it can be tempting to let your fingers get close to the blades when using the smaller hand spiralizers without using the clamp, which is useful for carrots and broccoli stems. I recommend a chef's wire cut-resistant glove if you use the hand spiralizer. These are available online and from chef's equipment stores.

Spiralizer blades that come with most spiralizers are well designed for attaching and detaching from the spiralizing mechanism without the risk of cutting your fingers.

However, you must be careful when you clean them and especially when you pull remnants of spiralized produce out of the blades. For cleaning, the best tool to use is an old-fashioned toothbrush. A round palm brush works, too, but I find that the toothbrush allows me to get into the small spaces between the blades most efficiently and safely while my fingers stay far away from the sharp parts. I now keep a dedicated toothbrush by the kitchen sink for this purpose alone. Wash all of the parts with warm water and detergent, and wash as soon as you finish spiralizing so the juices from the produce (especially beets) don't stain the spiralizer. The gadgets are light and easy to clean.

Salads

Sometimes spiralized vegetables are just too beautiful to cook. I found this to be the case time and again when I was working on the recipes for this book. I'd be preparing what I thought was going to be a pasta dish, and it would end up being a salad. I had no idea this chapter would be so big, with recipes that are adaptations of dishes from as far afield as Thailand and the Szechuan province of China, Morocco and France, Italy and Mexico.

The spiralizer is perfect for making crudité salads and slaws with carrots, beets, and radishes, and you'll find a few variations on them. I adapted two of my favorite French bistro salads, French Crudités Salad with Lentils in Mustard Vinaigrette (page 42) and Salade Niçoise (page 45), into spiralized recipes that make equally good starters or main-dish salads. I used the tool quite often for cucumbers, which have the most marvelous texture when sliced very thin and marinated in dressing. I've also made some great cucumber salads with cucumbers cut on the shredder and then snipped into smaller pieces, a task that in the past I would do with a grater or a food processor. The spiralizer is much quicker and neater.

In the spring I can get big watermelon radishes at my farmers market; they look like turnips on the outside, but inside they are the most beguiling dark mottled pink color, and when you spiralize them, whether on the shredder or the slicer blade, they are absolutely gorgeous. I'm sometimes tempted to forget about eating and wear the twisted strands made on the slicer blade as a necklace. But that wasn't the case only with the watermelon radishes. All spiralized food is a feast for the eyes, but salads are particularly beautiful.

Cucumbers Vinaigrette with Pickled Red Onions

Makes 4 to 6 servings

FOR THE RED ONIONS

1 medium red onion

Salt

1 dried bay leaf, broken into two pieces

2 garlic cloves, cut in half lengthwise, green shoots removed

3 tablespoons cider vinegar

3 tablespoons sherry vinegar

1 teaspoon sugar

FOR THE CUCUMBERS

1 large European cucumber or 2 regular cucumbers, peeled if desired

Salt

3 tablespoons champagne vinegar or sherry vinegar

½ to 1 teaspoon Dijon mustard (to taste)

Freshly ground black pepper

¼ cup grapeseed oil

2 tablespoons extra virgin olive oil

Optional: fresh parsley, dill, or chives, finely chopped

I have had a weakness for this French salad ever since I first tasted it on a terrace in Switzerland decades ago. I love the texture of the thinly sliced cucumbers bathed in vinaigrette. They are addictive. You will not need all of the pickled onions for this, but the extras are nice to have on hand.

SPIRALIZING THE RED ONION Use the shredder blade. Insert the onion into the spiralizer blade at the root end. Take up handfuls of the spiralized onion and cut into 2- to 3-inch lengths with scissors. 1 medium onion will yield about 1½ cups.

SPIRALIZING THE CUCUMBER Make a ½-inch incision down one side of the cucumber and spiralize using the slicer blade.

- To make the pickled onions, bring a medium pot of water to a boil and salt generously. Add the spiralized onion and blanch 45 seconds to 1 minute. Transfer to a bowl of cold water, then drain and rinse with cold water. Transfer to a medium bowl and add the remaining ingredients plus ½ teaspoon salt. Toss together. If the onions are not submerged in liquid, add a very small amount of water or add more vinegar. They should be just barely submerged. Cover the bowl and let stand for several hours, in or out of the refrigerator. Transfer to a jar and refrigerate if not using right away. They will keep for a week.

- Place the spiralized cucumber in a colander in the sink. Sprinkle with salt and let drain for 15 to 30 minutes. Transfer to a bowl.

- In a small bowl or measuring cup whisk together the vinegar, mustard, salt, and pepper. Whisk in the oils. Toss with the cucumbers and herbs, if using. Taste and adjust seasonings. Serve right away, or refrigerate for up to 30 minutes and serve. Garnish with pickled onions.

ADVANCE PREPARATION You can make this up to 30 minutes before serving. If dressing becomes watery, serve with a slotted spoon.

Cucumber Tzatziki

Makes 3 to 4 servings

1 large European cucumber or
  2 regular cucumbers, peeled
  if desired
  Salt
1½ cups Greek yogurt
2 to 3 garlic cloves, mashed
  in a mortar and pestle with
  ¼ teaspoon salt
2 tablespoons extra virgin
  olive oil
1 to 2 tablespoons chopped fresh
  mint or dill
1 tablespoon red wine vinegar

Tzatziki is one of my favorite Greek salads, a garlicky mix of cucumbers and thick Greek yogurt. Serve this as an appetizer, a side salad, or a dip.

SPIRALIZING THE CUCUMBER Make a ½-inch incision down one side of the cucumber. Use the shredder blade.

- Place the spiralized cucumbers in a colander in the sink. Sprinkle with salt and let drain for 15 to 30 minutes. Transfer to a bowl.

- Toss the cucumber with the yogurt and the remaining ingredients. Taste and adjust salt and garlic. Refrigerate until ready to serve.

ADVANCE PREPARATION Don't make this too far ahead, because the cucumbers will continue to release water into the tzatziki and the bright flavors will fade.

Hot and Sour Cucumber and Sprout Salad

Makes 4 to 6 servings

FOR THE SALAD

1½ European cucumbers or
   2 large regular cucumbers,
   peeled and trimmed

6 fat radishes, cut in julienne if
   too narrow to spiralize, plus
   additional fat radishes for
   garnish
   Salt

3 cups bean sprouts

3 scallions, both white and green
   parts, thinly sliced

¼ cup cilantro, chopped

1 tablespoon black sesame seeds
   Lettuce leaves for serving
   Radishes, spiralized on the
   slicer blade, for garnish

FOR THE DRESSING

2 tablespoons sesame tahini or
   crunchy peanut butter

1 tablespoon soy sauce

¼ cup seasoned rice vinegar

2 to 3 teaspoons hot spiced
   Chinese or Korean chile oil

⅛ to ¼ teaspoon cayenne, to
   taste

2 tablespoons dark sesame oil

2 to 3 teaspoons minced fresh
   ginger, to taste

1 large garlic clove, minced

½ cup grapeseed oil or canola oil

This is inspired by a wonderful salad I ate years ago at a Szechuan restaurant in San Francisco. The dressing is nutty and spicy, the cucumbers and sprouts crunchy and refreshing against its heat. Make sure to salt the cucumbers and let them drain for a while before assembling the salad so it won't be watery.

SPIRALIZING THE CUCUMBER Use the shredder blade. Take up handfuls of the spiralized cucumbers and cut into manageable lengths with scissors.

SPIRALIZING THE RADISHES If the radishes are fat, spiralize the 6 radishes for the salad on the shredder blade and slice the cores thin. Spiralize the garnish radishes on the slicer blade.

- Place the spiralized cucumbers in a colander in the sink. Sprinkle with salt and let drain for 15 to 30 minutes. Transfer to a bowl.

- In a large bowl combine the cucumbers, sprouts, scallions, cilantro, radishes, and sesame seeds.

- Combine the dressing ingredients in a small bowl and whisk together, or blend with an immersion blender until smooth. Toss with the salad mixture.

- Line a platter or wide bowl with lettuce leaves. Top with the salad and garnish with additional radishes.

ADVANCE PREPARATION The dressing will keep for 3 to 4 days in the refrigerator. Blend again before using.

Asian Zucchini Noodle Salad with Watermelon Radishes or Daikon

Makes 6 servings

FOR THE SALAD

- 1¾ pounds zucchini
- ½ pound watermelon radishes or daikon, peeled
- 1 large red bell pepper
- 1 large romaine heart
- 3 scallions, both green and white parts, cleaned and thinly sliced on the diagonal (optional)
- 1 cup coarsely chopped cilantro
- 1 to 2 serrano chiles, minced, to taste

FOR THE DRESSING

- ¼ cup fresh lime juice
- 2 tablespoons Thai fish sauce or 1 tablespoon soy sauce
- 1 teaspoon sugar
- 2 to 3 teaspoons finely minced or grated fresh ginger, to taste
- 1 garlic clove, finely minced or put through a press
  Pinch of cayenne, or to taste
- 2 tablespoons dark sesame oil
- 2 tablespoons grapeseed or canola oil

This is a particularly beautiful salad if you can find watermelon radishes, those turnip-size radishes with dark pink interiors. I spiralize them on the slicer to get wide, flowerlike rings and use them as a gorgeous topping for the mix of zucchini, romaine, cilantro, and red pepper tossed in an addictive fish sauce–spiked dressing. If you can't find watermelon radishes, use daikon.

SPIRALIZING THE ZUCCHINI Use the shredder blade. Take up handfuls of the spiralized zucchini and cut into manageable lengths with scissors.

SPIRALIZING THE WATERMELON RADISHES OR DAIKON Peel the radishes or daikon. Use the slicer blade. Take up handfuls of the spiralized radishes and cut into manageable lengths with scissors.

SPIRALIZING THE RED PEPPER Use the shredder blade. Insert the bottom end into the spiralizer tube and spiralize until you reach the seed pod. Cut into 2-inch lengths with scissors. Cut the section around the seed pod by hand into thin strips.

• Bring a large pot of water to a boil, salt generously, and add the zucchini noodles. Cook 1 minute and transfer to a bowl of cold water. Drain, then drain again in a paper towel-lined bowl. Transfer to a large salad bowl and add the spiralized red pepper.

- Cut the romaine heart in half, then slice crosswise into thin strips. Add to the zucchini noodles, along with the scallions, cilantro, and chile. Toss together.

- For the dressing, whisk together the lime juice, fish sauce or soy sauce, sugar, ginger, garlic, and cayenne. Whisk in the oils. Taste and adjust seasonings. Set aside 2 tablespoons and toss the rest with the salad mixture.

- Toss the radishes or daikon with the remaining 2 tablespoons dressing and arrange on top of the salad.

ADVANCE PREPARATION You can prepare the spiralized vegetables in Step 1 up to 2 days ahead and refrigerate.

Beet and Spinach Salad

Makes 4 servings

FOR THE SALAD

- 2 small beets or 1 medium beet, peeled and ends trimmed
- 1 teaspoon balsamic vinegar
- 2 teaspoons sherry vinegar
  Salt
- 1 tablespoon extra virgin olive oil
- 5 to 6 ounces stemmed, washed and dried fresh spinach, or 1 bag baby spinach
  Handful of coarsely chopped walnuts
- 1 ounce blue cheese, crumbled (about ¼ cup)
- 1 to 2 tablespoons minced chives, dill, parsley, or tarragon, to taste

FOR THE DRESSING

- 1 tablespoon plus 1 teaspoon fresh lemon juice or sherry vinegar (or a combination)
- 1 small garlic clove, put through a press or pureed
  Salt or fleur de sel
- 1 teaspoon Dijon mustard
- ¼ cup extra virgin olive oil

I love to cut beets on the slicer blade, resulting in very thin slices, and I find the best way to cook the spiralized beets is in the steamer. Just be sure to steam them for about 15 minutes so they soften properly; this brings out the maximum flavor. For this salad, I toss the steamed beets with a little bit of vinegar and oil, then combine them with fresh spinach, walnuts, and blue cheese.

SPIRALIZING THE BEETS Use the slicer blade. Take up handfuls of the spiralized beets and cut into smaller circles or half-moons. Wide beets may come off the blade in slices rather than long spirals.

● Bring 1 to 2 inches of water to boil in a steamer. Place the spiralized beets in the basket; cover and steam 15 minutes. Test for doneness. They should be tender to the bite and tasty. If they are al dente, steam for another 5 minutes. Remove from the heat and transfer to a bowl. Toss with the balsamic vinegar, the 2 teaspoons sherry vinegar, salt to taste, and the 1 tablespoon olive oil. Let cool.

● In a large salad bowl combine the spinach, walnuts, blue cheese, fresh herbs, and beets.

● In a small bowl or measuring cup whisk together the lemon juice or sherry vinegar, garlic, salt, and Dijon mustard. Whisk in the olive oil. Just before serving, toss dressing with the salad.

ADVANCE PREPARATION The beets can be cooked and marinated (Step 1) up to 3 days ahead.

Beet Salad with Chickpeas and Anchovy Dressing

Makes 4 servings

4 medium beets, peeled

4 anchovy fillets, soaked in water for 15 minutes, drained, rinsed, and dried on paper towels

1 to 2 small or medium garlic cloves, peeled, to taste

2 tablespoons red wine vinegar or sherry vinegar, more to taste

Salt

⅓ cup extra virgin olive oil

Freshly ground black pepper

1 (15-ounce) can chickpeas, drained and rinsed, or 1½ cups cooked chickpeas

2 tablespoons minced flat-leaf parsley

This is a colorful Provençal salad with an assertive, garlicky dressing made with mashed anchovies, vinegar, and olive oil. I toss the chickpeas and steamed beet slices with the dressing separately. Then I make a layer of the beets on a large platter and pile the chickpeas in the middle.

SPIRALIZING THE BEETS Use the slicer blade. Cut into rounds or shorter lengths with scissors.

● Place the spiralized beets in a steamer over 1 inch boiling water. Cover and steam 15 minutes or until tender.

● Mash together the anchovy fillets and garlic in a mortar and pestle until they are reduced to a paste. Add the vinegar and mix together well with the pestle or a fork. Add salt if desired. Work in the olive oil. Season with pepper.

● Place the chickpeas in a bowl and toss with 2 tablespoons of the dressing and 1 tablespoon of the parsley. Toss the beets with the remaining dressing and parsley in another bowl and arrange on a platter. Arrange the chickpeas on top.

ADVANCE PREPARATION Both the beets and the anchovies can be dressed ahead and will keep for up to 3 days in the refrigerator.

Shredded Beet and Watermelon Radish Slaw

Makes 6 servings

1 pound beets, peeled and trimmed

½ pound watermelon radishes, large regular radishes, or daikon radish

Salt

1 cup freshly squeezed orange juice or blood orange juice

2 tablespoons fresh lemon juice

3 tablespoons slivered mint leaves

Pinch of cinnamon

Romaine lettuce leaves for serving

The inspiration for this spiralized slaw is a North African salad that I love, a simple mix of shredded raw beets tossed with cinnamon-infused orange juice. I added radishes to the mix here. The beets soften after they are salted, and then a bit more as they marinate in the citrus juice. Blood orange juice is particularly good if you can get hold of blood oranges, which are more tart than regular oranges. There will be a lot of juice in the bowl after you've put this salad together. That's why I like to serve it over lettuce leaves.

SPIRALIZING THE BEETS Use the shredder blade. Take up handfuls of the spiralized beets and cut into 2-inch lengths with scissors.

SPIRALIZING THE RADISHES Peel watermelon radishes and daikon; no need to peel regular radishes. Use the shredder blade. Take up handfuls of the spiralized radishes and cut into 2-inch lengths with scissors.

• Toss the spiralized vegetables, together or separately, with salt and transfer to a colander. Set in the sink to drain for 15 to 30 minutes.

• Combine the orange and lemon juices. In a large bowl toss together the beets and radishes with the mint, cinnamon, and juices.

• Line a wide bowl or platter with lettuce leaves and top with the salad.

ADVANCE PREPARATION The salad will keep for a day in the refrigerator. There will be a lot of liquid in the bottom of the bowl, and you may want to discard some of it after tossing again with the salad.

Southeast Asian Carrot and Daikon Radish Slaw

Makes 4 servings

This mix of carrots, daikon, fresh herbs, and chiles tossed with a tart, pungent dressing is Thai through and through. I use the same mix to fill spring rolls (page 159).

FOR THE SALAD

- ½ pound daikon, peeled
- 1 pound fat carrots, peeled
- 1 to 2 serrano chiles, minced, to taste (optional)
- 3 tablespoons chopped fresh mint
- 2 tablespoons minced chives
- 2 tablespoons chopped Thai basil or tarragon
- ½ cup chopped cilantro

FOR THE DRESSING

- ¼ cup fresh lime juice
- 1 tablespoon Thai fish sauce or 2 to 3 teaspoons soy sauce
- 2 teaspoons sugar
- 2 to 3 teaspoons finely minced or grated fresh ginger, to taste
- 1 garlic clove, finely minced or put through a press
  Pinch of cayenne, more to taste
- 2 tablespoons dark sesame oil
- ¼ cup grapeseed or canola oil

SPIRALIZING THE DAIKON Use the shredder blade. Take up handfuls of the spiralized daikon and cut into 2-inch lengths with scissors. You should have about 2 cups.

SPIRALIZING THE CARROTS Use the shredder blade. Cut away the thinner end and spiralize the fat end. Take up handfuls of the spiralized carrots and cut into 2-inch lengths with scissors. You should have about 4 cups.

- Combine all of the salad ingredients in a bowl.

- Whisk together the lime juice, fish sauce or soy sauce, sugar, ginger, garlic, and cayenne. Whisk in oils. Taste and adjust seasonings. Toss with the salad mixture.

ADVANCE PREPARATION The salad will keep for a day in the refrigerator.

Jicama and Orange Salad

Makes 4 to 6 servings (more if used as a salsa)

1 medium jicama (about
  12 ounces), peeled

¼ cup fresh lime juice
  Salt

3 blood oranges or 2 navel
  oranges
  Pure ground medium-hot chili
  powder or chile pequín powder,
  to taste

2 tablespoons chopped cilantro

This refreshing mixture can serve as both a salad and a salsa. I use the coarse shredder for the jicama and, depending on its circumference, I get either coils or curved pieces, both of which I cut smaller with scissors. This beautiful, refreshing mixture can stand alone or garnish a taco. I particularly like this when I make it with blood oranges, but navels are great, too.

SPIRALIZING THE JICAMA Use the chipper (coarse shredder) blade. Take up handfuls of the spiralized jicama and cut into 3-inch lengths with scissors.

● Toss together the jicama, lime juice, and salt. Let sit at room temperature for 1 hour, tossing every so often.

● Cut the ends off the oranges. Stand on one end on a cutting board that has a lip for catching juice. Using a serrated knife or a sharp chef's knife, cut away the skin and pith by cutting down the sides of the orange from top to bottom. Remove sections by cutting between the membranes, and cut sections in half. Add to the jicama and tip in all of the juice on the board.

● Add the remaining ingredients and toss together. Let stand for at least 15 minutes, preferably 2 hours.

ADVANCE PREPARATION This will keep for a few hours in the refrigerator.

Moroccan Parsnip Salad

Makes 4 servings

1½ pounds very fat parsnips, trimmed and peeled

4 tablespoons extra virgin olive oil

2 large garlic cloves, minced or pureed in a mortar and pestle with ¼ teaspoon salt

½ teaspoon freshly ground black pepper

1 teaspoon cumin seeds, lightly toasted and ground

Salt

3 tablespoons fresh lemon juice, to taste

¼ cup chopped flat-leaf parsley

Imported black olives

2 hard-boiled eggs, cut in wedges (optional)

I modeled this sweet and pungent salad after one of my favorite North African carrot salads, ommok houria. Most carrots are not fat enough for the spiralizer, but I often find large, fat parsnips. I always core parsnips because the core is so woody, and the spiralizer makes this very easy! Parsnips have a sweet flavor that contrasts nicely with the aromatic garlic and lemon juice in this dish.

SPIRALIZING THE PARSNIPS Cut off the narrow end of the parsnip where it is narrower than the center of the spiralizer. Use the slicer blade. Take up handfuls of the spiralized parsnips and cut into manageable lengths with scissors.

- Heat 2 tablespoons of the olive oil over medium heat in a large, heavy skillet and add the spiralized parsnips. Cook, stirring often, until tender, about 8 to 10 minutes.

- Stir in the garlic, pepper, and cumin. Cook, stirring, for about 30 seconds, until the garlic is fragrant. Add salt to taste. Stir together for a few minutes, until the parsnips are nicely seasoned. Remove from the heat and stir in the lemon juice, remaining olive oil, and the parsley. Taste and adjust salt. Transfer to a platter, and garnish with olives and hard-boiled eggs, if desired. Serve at room temperature.

ADVANCE PREPARATION You can make this several hours before serving. Without the lemon juice and parsley, the dish will keep for a couple of days in the refrigerator. Reheat gently on top of the stove, and add the lemon juice and parsley.

Tuna and Bean Salad with Spiralized Cucumber

Makes 4 servings

1 small red onion, peeled

½ European cucumber or one regular cucumber, peeled if desired

2 tablespoons plus 1 teaspoon red wine vinegar or sherry vinegar

2 (5-ounce) cans water-packed or olive oil-packed tuna, drained

1 (15-ounce) can cannellini beans or borlotti beans, drained and rinsed

3 fresh sage leaves, slivered

2 tablespoons finely chopped flat-leaf parsley

1 anchovy fillet, rinsed

1 small or medium garlic clove

1 tablespoon fresh lemon juice

Salt and freshly ground black pepper

1 teaspoon Dijon mustard

⅓ cup extra virgin olive oil

This is based on a classic Italian salad that can be thrown together with pantry items. All you need from the market is the cucumber, which makes a beautiful garnish for the high-protein tuna-and-bean mix.

SPIRALIZING THE ONION Use the shredder blade. Insert the onion into the spiralizer blade at the root end. Take up handfuls of the spiralized onion and cut into 2- to 3-inch lengths with scissors.

SPIRALIZING THE CUCUMBER Use the slicer blade. Take up handfuls of the spiralized cucumber and cut into 2- to 3-inch lengths with scissors.

- Place the spiralized onion in a bowl and add 1 teaspoon of the vinegar and cold water to cover. Let stand for 5 minutes. Drain and rinse with cold water, then dry on paper towels.

- In a medium bowl or salad bowl combine the tuna, beans, onions, sage, and parsley.

- Mash together the anchovy and garlic in a mortar and pestle. Add the remaining vinegar, the lemon juice, salt to taste, freshly ground pepper, and Dijon mustard, and mix together. Whisk in the olive oil or work in with the pestle.

- Set aside 1 tablespoon of the dressing. Toss the rest with the tuna and beans. Toss the spiralized cucumbers with the remaining dressing. Arrange the tuna-and-beans salad in a bowl or on a platter, and top with the cucumbers.

ADVANCE PREPARATION The tuna-and-beans salad, without the cucumbers, will keep for a couple of days in the refrigerator.

French Crudités Salad with Lentils in Mustard Vinaigrette

Makes 4 to 6 servings

FOR THE SALAD

2 medium beets, peeled and trimmed

2 large fat carrots, peeled

1 European cucumber or 2 regular cucumbers, peeled if desired

¾ cup brown or green lentils (6 ounces)

½ yellow onion

2 garlic cloves, peeled and crushed

1 bay leaf

Salt

2 tablespoons minced fresh chives

2 tablespoons chopped fresh parsley

2 to 3 ripe tomatoes or a half box of cherry tomatoes, in season only, cut in wedges or sliced

Freshly ground black pepper

FOR THE VINAIGRETTE

3 tablespoons sherry vinegar

1 small garlic clove, put through a press or mashed in a mortar and pestle

Salt

1 tablespoon Dijon mustard

⅓ cup extra virgin olive oil

3 tablespoons grapeseed oil

This is a typical French café lunch—a plate of mixed crudités (carrots, cucumbers, beets, tomatoes in season), often with lentils thrown into the mix, dressed with a mustardy vinaigrette. Here, the vegetables are spiralized, which is a beautiful way to present this healthy, satisfying meal.

SPIRALIZING THE BEETS AND CARROTS Use the shredder blade. Take up handfuls of the spiralized beets and carrots and cut into manageable lengths with scissors.

SPIRALIZING THE CUCUMBER Use the slicer blade. Take up handfuls of the spiralized cucumber and cut into manageable lengths with scissors.

● Rinse the lentils and place in a saucepan. Add 1 quart water, the onion half, crushed garlic cloves, and bay leaf. Bring to a gentle boil; reduce heat to low, cover, and simmer 20 minutes. Add salt to taste (I use a teaspoon or more) and continue to simmer 15 to 20 minutes more until just tender but not mushy. Using tongs, remove the half onion, garlic cloves, and bay leaf. Remove the lentils from the heat and drain through a strainer (you can place the strainer over a bowl and use the tasty broth for another purpose).

● Meanwhile, place the spiralized beets in a steamer set over 1 inch of boiling water and steam for 15 to 20 minutes, until tender. Remove from the heat.

● For vinaigrette, in a bowl or measuring cup whisk together the vinegar, mashed garlic, salt, and mustard. Whisk in the oils. Taste and adjust seasoning.

● Toss the lentils with ¼ cup of the vinaigrette, 2 teaspoons of the chives, and 2 teaspoons of the parsley.

● One at a time, toss the spiralized carrots, the spiralized cucumber, and the tomatoes separately with 2 tablespoons vinaigrette and some chives and parsley. Arrange the lentils and vegetables on a platter or on individual plates. Grind some pepper over all of the crudités.

ADVANCE PREPARATION The lentils can be cooked and dressed up to 4 days ahead and kept in the refrigerator. The carrots and beets can be prepped and dressed a day ahead, but do not add the herbs until shortly before serving. The dressing will keep for a week in the refrigerator.

Spiralized Niçoise Salad

Makes 4 servings

This niçoise salad is somewhat deconstructed. It's so nice to see the curls of spiralized vegetables. But don't hesitate to toss it all together once friends have had a good look.

FOR THE VINAIGRETTE

- 2 tablespoons red wine vinegar or sherry vinegar
- 1 tablespoon fresh lemon juice
- 1 small garlic clove, put through a press or mashed in a mortar and pestle
- Salt and freshly ground black pepper
- 2 teaspoons Dijon mustard
- ½ cup extra virgin olive oil

FOR THE SALAD

- ¾ to 1 pound medium-size Yukon gold or red bliss potatoes, peeled if desired
- 1 red or green bell pepper
- 2 fat carrots, peeled
- ½ European cucumber or 1 regular cucumber, peeled if waxy
- 1 (5-ounce) can olive oil-packed or water-packed tuna, drained
- 1 small head Boston lettuce, romaine heart, or 4 to 5 cups mixed baby salad greens, washed and dried
- 2 to 4 tablespoons chopped fresh herbs, such as parsley, basil, tarragon, chives, or marjoram
- 6 ounces green beans, trimmed and cut in half if long, blanched or steamed for 4 to 5 minutes
- 2 to 3 ripe tomatoes, in season only, or half a box of cherry tomatoes
- 2 hard-cooked eggs, peeled and cut in wedges
- 6 to 8 anchovy fillets, drained and rinsed
- Imported black olives

SPIRALIZING THE POTATOES

Use the chipper (coarse shredder) blade. Take up handfuls of the spiralized potatoes and cut into manageable lengths with scissors.

SPIRALIZING THE PEPPER

Use the chipper (coarse shredder) blade. Insert the bottom end into the spiralizer tube and spiralize until you reach the seed pod. When you reach the seed pod, remove pepper from the spiralizer and cut the remaining flesh (about one-third of the pepper) away from the seed pod. Slice crosswise the same thickness as the spiralized portion. Take up handfuls of the spiralized pepper and cut into 2- to 3-inch lengths with scissors.

SPIRALIZING THE CARROTS

Use the shredder blade. Take up handfuls of the spiralized carrots and cut into manageable lengths with scissors.

SPIRALIZING THE CUCUMBER

Use the slicer blade. Take up handfuls of the spiralized cucumber and cut into manageable lengths with scissors.

- In a small bowl whisk together the vinegar, lemon juice, garlic, salt and pepper to taste, and Dijon mustard. Whisk in the olive oil.

- Steam the spiralized potatoes above 1 inch simmering water for 5 minutes, until tender. Transfer to a large salad bowl and season with salt and pepper. Add the tuna, and while the potatoes are hot toss with ¼ cup of the vinaigrette.

- In a large bowl combine the salad greens and half the fresh herbs, and toss with 3 tablespoons of the vinaigrette. Pile onto a platter. One at a time, toss the spiralized peppers, carrots, cucumber, and green beans with equal amounts of the remaining vinaigrette and arrange on the platter. Garnish with tomatoes, eggs, anchovies, and olives.

ADVANCE PREPARATION The potatoes can be cooked and tossed with the dressing and tuna a day ahead.

Soups and Noodle Bowls

Most of the recipes in this chapter are noodle bowls, with spiralized vegetables standing in for the traditional Asian noodles. I cook the spiralized vegetable noodles separately, distribute them among bowls, and top them with vegetables, usually some form of protein (tofu, fish, chicken), and a comforting broth for a simple and surprisingly filling meal.

If you want to work ahead on the noodle bowls, the broths keep well in the refrigerator for a few days or in the freezer for months, or you can use commercial broths. The spiralized noodles keep well for a couple of days in the refrigerator before you cook them and will keep for a day after you cook them.

I also use the spiralizer for a classic, hearty Italian minestrone (page 59), with winter squash noodles standing in for the pasta that is traditionally added to this soup shortly before cooking. You can make the same soup in the summer with zucchini noodles, and you can use the spiralizer to prep some of the other vegetables in the soup, like the onion and the turnip.

In fact, you might want to try the spiralizer for some of your other favorite soups, just to help you with vegetable prep. It would be great, for instance, for a classic French onion soup, saving you the task of slicing all those onions. You can also spiralize pretty garnishes, especially for cold soups in the summer—a twist of cucumber with your favorite gazpacho, a few spirals of zucchini on a cold summer squash soup. There are endless possibilities.

Vegetarian Phô with Turnip and Zucchini Noodles

Makes 6 servings

Vietnamese phô is traditionally made with meat and aromatics. I've developed a vegetarian version that I find as delicious as authentic phô and much easier to make. The aromatics—scorched onion and ginger, star anise, cloves, cinnamon, and peppercorns—are the same, and that's what makes this dish so fragrant. Spiralized vegetable noodles stand in for traditional rice noodles for a nutrition-packed meal in a bowl.

FOR THE BROTH

- 1 large onion (about ½ pound), peeled and quartered
- 1 3-inch piece fresh ginger
- 3 quarts water
- 1 pound leeks (1½ large), tough ends cut away, halved, cleaned, and cut in thick slices
- 1½ pounds carrots, peeled and sliced thick
- 2 ounces shiitake or white mushroom stems (from about 8 ounces mushrooms; save caps for soup if desired), or 4 dried shiitakes
- 1 head garlic, halved
- 2 stalks lemongrass, trimmed, smashed with the side of a knife, and sliced
  Salt
- 1 to 1½ tablespoons raw brown sugar (to taste)
- 6 star anise pods
- 5 whole cloves
- 1 tablespoon black peppercorns
- 1 2- to 3-inch cinnamon stick
- 1 to 2 tablespoons Thai fish sauce or soy sauce, to taste (optional)

FOR THE SOUP

- 1 14-ounce box firm tofu, drained and diced
- 1 pound turnips or rutabaga, peeled
- 1 pound zucchini
  Sliced caps from the 8 ounces mushrooms (optional)
- 3 shallots, sliced paper-thin, separated into rings, and soaked for 5 minutes in cold water, then drained and rinsed
- 4 scallions, white and dark green parts, chopped
- 1 cup chopped cilantro
- ½ cup Asian or purple basil leaves, slivered
- 2 cups mung bean sprouts
- 2 to 4 bird or serrano chiles, finely chopped, to taste
  Several sprigs fresh mint
- 3 to 4 limes, cut in wedges

SPIRALIZING THE TURNIPS (OR RUTABAGA) AND ZUCCHINI

Use the shredder blade. Take up handfuls and cut long strands into manageable lengths with scissors.

- Scorch the onion and ginger by holding the pieces above a flame with tongs, or in a dry frying pan if using an electric stove. Turn the pieces until scorched black in places on all sides. Slice the ginger lengthwise.

- Combine the scorched onion and ginger with the water, leeks, carrots, mushroom stems or dried shiitakes, garlic, lemongrass, salt to taste, and sugar in a large soup pot and bring to a boil. Tie the star anise, cloves, peppercorns, and cinnamon stick in a cheesecloth bag and add to the soup. Reduce the heat, cover, and simmer for 1 hour. Add the fish sauce or soy sauce, and simmer for 20 minutes. Strain through a cheesecloth-lined strainer into a bowl and then return to the pot. Taste and adjust salt and sugar.

continued on page 50

continued from page 48

• Add the tofu to the broth and simmer 20 minutes. Add the sliced mushroom caps (is using).

• Bring a separate pot of water to a boil, salt generously, and add the turnip or rutabaga noodles. Cook 1 to 1½ minutes, and transfer to a bowl of cold water using tongs or a skimmer. Drain. Add the zucchini noodles to the boiling water and cook 1 to 1½ minutes. Transfer to a bowl of cold water, drain, and toss with the turnip noodles.

• Divide the turnip and zucchini noodles among six large soup bowls. Ladle in a generous amount of hot broth. Sprinkle on the shallots, scallions, and half of the cilantro and basil. Pass the bean sprouts, chopped chiles, the remaining cilantro and basil, the mint sprigs, and lime wedges. Serve with chopsticks for the noodles and soup spoons for the broth.

ADVANCE PREPARATION The broth will keep for a few days in the refrigerator and can be frozen. The noodles can be cooked several hours ahead. Keep in a bowl. Just before serving, reheat by dunking briefly into a pot of simmering water and draining (it helps to place them in a strainer or pasta pot insert).

VARIATION Add cooked shredded chicken breast to each serving.

Kombu Mushroom Broth

Makes 6 cups

6 dried shiitake mushrooms or a
small handful of dried porcinis
or other dried mushrooms

1 bunch scallions, sliced

1 4- to 6-inch stick kombu

1 medium carrot, sliced thin
Handful of mushroom stems,
or a couple of dried shiitakes

7 cups water

2 to 3 tablespoons soy sauce,
to taste

1 to 2 tablespoons rice wine
(mirin), to taste (optional)
Salt
Sugar (optional)

This is based on a stock in Deborah Madison's Vegetarian Cooking for
Everybody. *You can use dried shiitakes or porcinis to get the rich mushroom
flavor. Porcinis yield a more robust broth; shiitakes are lighter.*

● Combine all the ingredients except the salt and sugar in a saucepan and
bring to a simmer. Cover and simmer 20 minutes. Strain. Season to taste
with salt and a pinch of sugar if desired.

Broccoli Stem Noodle Bowl with Broccoli and Smoked Trout

Makes 4 servings

2 bunches broccoli with thick stems, florets separated from stems (use only florets from one bunch and set aside the florets from the other for another purpose)

7 cups Kombu Mushroom Broth (page 51), chicken stock, or vegetable stock

Soy sauce or salt to taste

½ pound smoked trout fillets, cut into four 2-ounce pieces

1 bunch scallions, thinly sliced, white, light green, and dark green parts kept separate

Broccoli stems make delicious spiralized noodles. You can only make this if you can find broccoli with thick enough stems to go through the spiralizer, and a hand spiralizer is easiest for the job. The soup makes a satisfying meal in a bowl.

SPIRALIZING THE BROCCOLI STEMS Trim away the bottoms of the broccoli stems. Trim away the floret ends. Using a paring knife, peel away skin, which should come off stems in strips if you set the knife between skin and stem and ease it away. Use the shredder blade. Take up handfuls of the spiralized broccoli and cut long strands into manageable lengths with scissors.

● Bring a large pot of water to a boil, salt generously, and add the spiralized broccoli stems. Boil 1 minute and transfer to a bowl of cold water, then drain. Distribute among four bowls.

● Bring the broth to a simmer. Taste and adjust seasoning, adding soy sauce or salt if desired. Cut broccoli florets from 1 bunch broccoli into ¼-inch-thick slices. Add to the stock and simmer uncovered for 3 minutes. Add trout pieces and the white and light green parts of the scallions to the broth. Cover tightly and turn off the heat. Let stand for 3 minutes.

● Set a piece of trout on top of the broccoli-stem noodles in each bowl. Ladle in the soup, taking care to distribute the broccoli florets and scallions evenly. Sprinkle the dark green part of the scallions over each serving.

ADVANCE PREPARATION The broccoli stem noodles can be cooked ahead and kept in the refrigerator for a couple of days. The broth can also be made a day or two ahead.

Zucchini Noodle Bowl with Chicken and Spinach

Makes 4 to 6 servings

1½ to 2 pounds zucchini

3 pounds chicken pieces (on the bone), or 1 pound boneless, skinless chicken breasts

1 onion, quartered

1 piece ginger root, about 2 inches long, peeled and sliced

4 garlic cloves, peeled

1 teaspoon peppercorns
Salt

2 tablespoons Thai fish sauce

1 bunch spinach, stemmed and washed twice

1 cup chopped cilantro

2 limes, cut into wedges

When you poach the chicken for this noodle bowl, you are making the broth at the same time. The soup has Thai overtones with the fish sauce, cilantro, and the squeeze of lime at the end.

SPIRALIZING THE ZUCCHINI Use the shredder blade. Take up handfuls of the spiralized zucchini and cut long strands into manageable lengths with scissors.

● Make the broth. If possible, do this step a day ahead. Combine the chicken and 3 quarts water in a large, heavy soup pot and bring to a simmer. Skim off foam and add the onion, ginger root, garlic cloves, peppercorn, and 1 teaspoon salt. Reduce the heat, cover partially, and simmer 40 minutes for chicken pieces on the bone, 20 minutes for chicken breasts. Skim occasionally. Remove the chicken from the broth and let cool. If you use chicken breasts, simmer the broth for another 40 minutes.

● Line a strainer with cheesecloth and strain the broth into a bowl. Refrigerate the broth overnight or for at least 3 hours. Lift off the fat from the surface and discard.

● When the chicken is cool enough to handle, shred and refrigerate in a covered container until ready to serve the soup.

● About 30 minutes before you wish to serve, remove the chicken and broth from the refrigerator. Bring the broth to a simmer and add the fish sauce and salt to taste. Taste and adjust seasonings.

● Bring a large pot of water to a boil. Add the zucchini noodles and cook 1½ minutes. Drain and set aside.

● Just before serving, add the spinach leaves to the simmering soup. To serve the soup, distribute the zucchini noodles among four to six large bowls. Top with shredded chicken and a handful of cilantro. Ladle the simmering broth, with some of the spinach, into each bowl over the chicken and noodles. Serve at once, passing the limes for guests to squeeze on as they wish. You might not use all of the chicken. Add leftovers to salads.

ADVANCE PREPARATION The broth can (and should) be made the day before you make the soup. It can be made up to 3 days ahead.

Zucchini Noodle Bowl with Tofu, Shiitakes, and Mizuna

Makes 4 servings

1½ to 2 pounds zucchini

1 ounce dried mushrooms, either shiitakes or porcinis

½ pound fresh shiitake mushrooms

½ pound fresh button or cremini mushrooms, quartered

1 head garlic, halved crosswise

Salt to taste (about 2 teaspoons)

6 slices fresh ginger, from the widest part of the root

2 tablespoons soy sauce

14 to 16 ounces tofu (1 box), either firm or soft, cut in 1-inch dice

2 cups mizuna or baby arugula

½ cup chopped cilantro

This is one of my favorite noodle bowls. The tofu absorbs the deep flavors of the mushroom broth and develops a marvelous spongy texture after simmering in the broth. I love the texture of the abundant mushrooms and the bite and freshness of the feathery greens.

SPIRALIZING THE ZUCCHINI Use the shredder blade. Take up handfuls of the spiralized zucchini and cut long strands into manageable lengths using a scissors.

• Place the dried mushrooms in a bowl or large heatproof measuring cup and cover with 2 cups boiling water. Let sit for 30 minutes. If mushrooms are sandy, agitate from time to time. Line a strainer with cheesecloth and place over a 1-quart measuring cup. Drain mushrooms through the strainer, then twist in the cheesecloth, holding them over the strainer, to squeeze out the last of the flavorful liquid. Discard reconstituted mushrooms or set aside for another use.

• While porcinis are soaking, pull the tough stems away from the fresh shiitake mushroom caps. Thinly slice the caps and set aside. Combine the dried mushroom broth with enough water to make 9 cups liquid, and place in a saucepan or soup pot. Add the quartered button or cremini mushrooms, the shiitake stems, the garlic, salt, and ginger slices, and bring to a boil. Reduce the heat, cover, and simmer 30 minutes.

• Use a slotted spoon or skimmer to remove all the solids (mushrooms, stems, garlic, and ginger) from broth. Add soy sauce. Taste and adjust salt.

• Bring the broth back to a boil and add the tofu. Reduce the heat to low, cover partially, and simmer for 30 minutes.

• Meanwhile, bring another pot of water to a boil, salt generously, and add the zucchini noodles. Cook 1 to 1½ minutes and drain. Distribute among four wide or deep soup bowls. Divide the mizuna or arugula among bowls.

• Add the thinly sliced shiitake mushroom caps to the simmering soup, cover, and simmer 5 minutes. Stir in the cilantro. Taste and adjust seasoning. Ladle the soup over the zucchini noodles and greens.

ADVANCE PREPARATION The broth can be prepared through Step 3 and refrigerated for 3 days or frozen for 2 months. The soup can be prepared through Step 4 a day ahead of time.

Minestrone with Winter Squash

Makes 6 servings

1 medium butternut squash

2 tablespoons extra virgin olive oil

1 medium onion, peeled and chopped

1 large or 2 medium carrots, peeled and diced (½-inch dice or smaller if desired)

1 celery stalk, diced (½-inch pieces or smaller if desired)

2 tablespoons chopped fresh parsley

Salt

2 leeks, white and light green parts only, halved, cleaned well, and sliced thin

3 to 4 garlic cloves, minced

1 (14- or 28-ounce) can chopped tomatoes, with juice

½ teaspoon dried thyme or 1 teaspoon chopped fresh thyme

2 turnips, peeled and diced or spiralized on the coarse blade and cut into smaller pieces

Bouquet garni made with a Parmesan rind, a bay leaf, and a couple sprigs each of parsley and thyme (omit Parmesan rind for a vegan soup)

1 (15-ounce) can cannellini beans or chickpeas, drained and rinsed well

Freshly ground black pepper

Freshly grated Parmesan

This is a classic minestrone, a hearty Mediterranean vegetable-and-bean soup, with spiralized winter squash standing in for the pasta that is traditionally added shortly before serving.

SPIRALIZING THE SQUASH Cut the straight neck of the squash away from the round bulbous part. Peel both parts using a Y-shape vegetable peeler. Cut the bottom bulbous section in half lengthwise, and scrape out the seeds and membranes; dice and set aside. Spiralize the long section using the chipper (coarse shredder) blade. Take up handfuls of the spiralized squash and cut into 3- or 4-inch lengths with scissors.

● Heat the olive oil over medium-low heat in a large, heavy soup pot or Dutch oven, and add the onion, carrots, celery, and parsley. Cook, stirring, until beginning to soften, about 3 minutes, and add a pinch of salt. Continue to cook, stirring often, a few more minutes until just about tender. Add the leeks and cook, stirring, until they begin to soften, about 3 minutes. Add the garlic and stir together until fragrant, 30 seconds to a minute, and stir in the tomatoes and thyme. Cook, stirring, until the tomatoes have cooked down and smell fragrant, about 10 minutes.

● Stir in 2 quarts water, the turnips, the diced winter squash, and the bouquet garni, and bring to a simmer. Add salt to taste (about 2 teaspoons), reduce the heat to low, cover, and simmer 45 minutes. Stir in the beans. Taste and adjust salt. Remove the bouquet garni.

● Add the spiralized winter squash to the soup and simmer another 5 to 10 minutes, until the squash strands are just cooked through. Grind in some pepper, and taste and adjust seasonings. The broth should be savory and rich-tasting. Serve with freshly grated Parmesan.

ADVANCE PREPARATION This keeps for 3 or 4 days in the refrigerator.

Frittatas, Gratins, and Other Egg Dishes

Egg dishes—frittatas, gratins, kugels, and the like—are an important part of my repertoire. This is in part because I love eggs, but also because they make such perfect vehicles for vegetables.

No matter the season, I probably make a vegetable gratin or frittata of one sort or another at least once a week. If I've got a few pounds of squash—winter or summer—lingering in my refrigerator, you can be sure that a squash gratin will show up at my table. If I've come home from the market with a few pounds of greens, they too will certainly show up in a frittata or gratin.

With the spiralizer I can now prep the vegetables for those dishes very quickly, and they will be uniform and beautiful. If I want to get ahead, I'll spiralize the vegetables and keep them in the refrigerator until I'm ready to make my dish. I won't think twice about adding some beautiful color to a greens frittata with a pan full of sautéed pepper strips garnishing the top (page 66), or for that matter, cooking up a big pepper stew to stir into scrambled eggs (page 82).

These dishes are simple enough for weeknight dinners but beautiful and substantial enough for a dinner party. I serve them as vegetarian main dishes, but you could also serve them as starters or sides. The frittatas, cut into diamond shapes, make particularly nice appetizers. They are among the most comforting dishes in this collection.

Zucchini and Red Pepper Frittata

Makes 6 main-dish servings, 12 appetizer servings

1 pound zucchini

1 large red bell pepper

2 tablespoons extra virgin olive oil

2 bunches scallions, white and light green parts only, trimmed and cut in thin slices

1 to 2 large garlic cloves, minced
Salt and freshly ground black pepper

8 large or extra-large eggs

2 tablespoons milk

¼ cup freshly grated Parmesan

2 tablespoons minced flat-leaf parsley

Because zucchini yields a fair amount of water after it's cooked, you will get the best texture if you make the filling a day ahead and let it drain overnight in the refrigerator. That said, I make this dish often on a whim because it's so easy to prep the vegetables with the spiralizer, without draining the zucchini filling, and it is still a wonderful frittata.

SPIRALIZING THE ZUCCHINI Use the chipper (coarse shredder) blade. Take up handfuls of the spiralized zucchini and cut into 2-inch lengths with scissors. Or make a ½-inch incision down one side of the squash to get half-moons.

SPIRALIZING THE RED PEPPER Use the shredder blade. Insert the bottom end into the spiralizer tube and spiralize until you reach the seed pod. When you reach the seed pod, remove the pepper from the spiralizer and cut the remaining flesh (about one-third of the pepper) away from the seed pod. Slice crosswise, the same thickness as the spiralized portion. Take up handfuls of the spiralized pepper and cut long strands into 2-inch lengths with scissors.

• Heat 1 tablespoon of the olive oil in a heavy 10-inch frying pan over medium heat and add the scallions and spiralized red pepper. Cook, stirring often, until the scallions are tender and the red pepper is beginning to soften. Add the garlic, salt, a few twists of the pepper mill, and the spiralized zucchini, and continue to cook for 3 to 5 minutes, until the pepper and zucchini are tender. Stir often. Remove from the heat and scrape into a bowl, or if working a day ahead, transfer to a strainer set over a bowl and refrigerate, uncovered, for several hours or overnight. Rinse and dry the pan.

• Beat the eggs in a large bowl. Stir in ½ teaspoon salt, some freshly ground pepper, the milk, Parmesan, parsley, and the cooked vegetables.

• Heat the remaining olive oil over medium-high heat in the skillet. Hold your hand above it; it should feel hot. Drop a bit of egg into the pan, and if it sizzles and cooks at once, the pan is ready. Pour in the egg mixture. Swirl the pan to distribute the eggs and filling evenly over the surface. Shake the pan gently, tilting it slightly while lifting up the edges of the frittata with the spatula, to let the eggs run underneath during the first few minutes of cooking.

• Turn the heat down to low, cover (use a pizza pan if you don't have a lid that will fit your skillet), and cook 10 minutes. From time to time remove the lid and loosen the bottom of the frittata with a wooden spatula, tilting the pan so the bottom doesn't burn. It will, however, turn a deep golden brown. The eggs should be just about set; cook a few minutes longer if they're not. Meanwhile, light the broiler.

• Finish the frittata under the broiler for 1 to 3 minutes, watching very carefully to make sure the top doesn't burn (at most it should brown very slightly, and it will puff under the broiler). Remove from the heat, shake the pan to make sure the frittata isn't sticking, and allow it to cool for 5 to 15 minutes. Loosen the edges with a wooden or plastic spatula. Carefully slide from the pan onto a large round platter. Cut into wedges or bite-size diamonds. Serve warm, at room temperature, or cold.

ADVANCE PREPARATION The filling can be prepared a day or two before making the frittata and held in a covered bowl in the refrigerator. The frittata can be made several hours ahead of serving, or a day ahead if serving cold. It does not reheat well.

Tunisian Carrot and Potato Frittata

Makes 6 to 8 servings

10 ounces (2 medium) moderately starchy potatoes, such as Yukon gold, scrubbed and peeled if desired

¾ pound fat carrots, peeled and trimmed

3 tablespoons extra virgin olive oil

Salt and freshly ground black pepper

2 large garlic cloves, mashed with a pinch of salt in a mortar and pestle, or finely chopped

2 teaspoons caraway seeds, half ground, half crushed

1 teaspoon ground cumin

8 large eggs

1 tablespoon harissa dissolved in 2 tablespoons water, or ¼ to ½ teaspoon cayenne

¼ cup finely chopped flat-leaf parsley

¼ cup chopped cilantro (or use ½ cup chopped parsley total)

When I went to Tunisia years ago, the frittatas were a revelation. They were filled with vegetables, and sometimes tuna, flavored with wonderfully aromatic spices like caraway, cumin, and spicy harissa, the chile paste that flavors many Tunisian dishes. This baked frittata is inspired by several Tunisian classics.

SPIRALIZING THE POTATOES Trim the potatoes at both ends. Make two incisions down two sides of the potatoes, approximately ½ inch deep, so they will spiralize as half-circles. Use the chipper (coarse shredder) blade. Slice the center stick ½ inch thick. You should have about 2 cups.

SPIRALIZING THE CARROTS Cut off the end of the carrot that is too narrow for the spiralizer, and slice that part in ½-inch rounds. Make lengthwise incisions on either side of the fat ends. Use the slicer blade to get half-circles. Slice the center stick ½ inch thick.

● Preheat the oven to 350 degrees.

● Heat a well-seasoned 9-inch cast-iron pan over medium-high heat for 1 to 2 minutes. Add 2 tablespoons of the olive oil and the spiralized potatoes and carrots. Cook, stirring often, for 3 to 5 minutes, until the vegetables begin to color slightly. Season with salt and pepper; turn heat to medium, cover, and continue to cook, stirring and scraping the bottom of the pan from time to time, for another 5 to 7 minutes, until the vegetables are tender. Stir in the garlic, caraway, and cumin, and cook, stirring, for another minute. Scrape the bottom of the pan to make sure the vegetables don't stick.

● Meanwhile, in a large bowl whisk the eggs and add ½ teaspoon salt, the harissa or cayenne, and the parsley and cilantro.

● If the pan is no longer hot, reheat over medium-high heat, stirring the vegetables. Add the remaining 1 tablespoon olive oil and pour in the eggs. Even out the mixture with a spatula and place in the oven. Bake 25 to 30 minutes, until lightly colored on the top and set. Let cool for 10 minutes or longer before serving. Serve warm or at room temperature.

ADVANCE PREPARATION You can make this a day ahead. Refrigerate, covered, and bring to room temperature before serving.

10-Egg Swiss Chard Frittata with Red Pepper Topping

Makes 8 to 10 main-dish servings, 12 to 16 appetizer servings

1 large red bell pepper

1¼ to 1½ pounds (2 generous bunches) Swiss chard, stemmed and washed thoroughly twice (about 8 cups tightly packed greens)

Salt

4 tablespoons extra virgin olive oil

3 garlic cloves, minced

2 teaspoons chopped fresh rosemary, or 1 teaspoon crumbled dried rosemary

2 teaspoons chopped fresh thyme, or 1 teaspoon dried thyme

Freshly ground black pepper

10 eggs

3 tablespoons milk

I top this classic Provençal frittata with spiralized red peppers, which provide not only a beautiful surface but a sweet flavor contrast to the herbal, garlicky filling. I make this for a crowd and cut it into diamond shapes. It makes a great hors d'oeuvre or main dish, perfect for a brunch.

SPIRALIZING THE PEPPER Use the chipper (coarse shredder) blade. Insert the bottom end into the spiralizer tube, and spiralize until you reach the seedpod. Remove from the spiralizer, and cut the remaining pepper flesh into thin strips by hand. Take up handfuls of the spiralized pepper and cut into 2- to 3-inch lengths with scissors.

• Heat a large pot of water over high heat while you stem and wash the chard in two changes of water. When the water in the pot comes to a boil, salt generously and add the chard. Cook 1 to 2 minutes, until just tender, and transfer to a bowl of cold water. Drain and take up by the handful to squeeze dry. Chop coarsely or cut into thin strips.

• Heat 1 tablespoon of the oil in a heavy 10- or 12-inch skillet over medium heat, and add two of the garlic cloves, the rosemary, and thyme. Cook, stirring, until fragrant, 30 seconds to a minute, and stir in the chard. Cook, stirring, for about 1 minute, until coated with oil. Season to taste with salt and pepper, and remove from the heat.

• Heat another tablespoon of olive oil in the skillet over medium heat, and add the remaining garlic and the spiralized red pepper. Cook, stirring often, until the pepper strips are tender, 5 to 8 minutes. Season to taste with salt and pepper. Transfer to a strainer set over a bowl to drain.

• Beat the eggs in a large bowl. Stir in ½ teaspoon salt (or more, to taste), freshly ground pepper to taste, the milk, and the cooked greens.

• Clean and dry your pan, and return it to the stove. Heat over medium-high heat and add the remaining olive oil. Hold your hand over the pan, and when you can feel the heat of the olive oil, test the heat by dropping a bit of egg into the pan. If it sizzles and cooks at once, the pan is ready. Pour in the egg mixture. Swirl the pan to distribute the eggs and filling evenly over the surface. Shake the pan gently, tilting it slightly while lifting up the edges of the frittata with the spatula to let the eggs run underneath during the first few minutes of cooking.

● Spread the peppers in an even layer over the top of the frittata. Turn the heat down to low, cover (use a pizza pan if you don't have a lid that will fit your skillet), and cook 10 to 12 minutes, shaking the pan gently every once in a while. From time to time, remove the lid and loosen the bottom of the frittata with a wooden spatula, tilting the pan so the bottom doesn't burn. It will, however, turn a deep golden brown. The eggs should be just about set; cook a few minutes longer if they're not. Meanwhile, heat the broiler.

● Finish the frittata under the broiler for 2 to 3 minutes, watching very carefully to make sure the top doesn't burn (it should brown slightly, and it will puff under the broiler). Remove from the heat, shake the pan to make sure the omelet isn't sticking (it will slide around a bit in the nonstick pan), and let cool for 5 to 15 minutes. Loosen the edges with a wooden or rubber spatula. Carefully slide from the pan onto a large round platter. Cut into wedges or diamonds.

ADVANCE PREPARATION The frittata can be made up to a day ahead and served at room temperature.

Frittata with Grated Zucchini, Goat Cheese, and Dill

Makes 6 servings

1¼ pounds zucchini

2 tablespoons extra virgin olive oil

2 garlic cloves, minced

Salt and freshly ground black pepper

8 eggs

3 ounces goat cheese, crumbled (about ¾ cup)

¼ cup chopped fresh dill

Goat cheese adds creaminess and rich flavor to this delicate frittata. When using cooked spiralized zucchini in egg preparations, it is best to let the cooked zucchini drain in a strainer set over a bowl for several hours—preferably overnight—so the zucchini doesn't dilute the eggs.

SPIRALIZING THE ZUCCHINI Use the shredder blade. Take up handfuls of the spiralized zucchini and cut long strands into 3-inch lengths with scissors.

- Heat 1 tablespoon of the oil over medium heat in a 10-inch heavy skillet, and add the spiralized zucchini. Cook, stirring, until the zucchini begins to wilt, about 2 minutes, and stir in the garlic. Cook for another minute, or just until the zucchini has wilted. It should still be bright green. Season to taste with salt and pepper, and remove from the heat. Transfer to a strainer, and set the strainer over a bowl. Let the zucchini drain for at least 1 hour, or refrigerate overnight, uncovered.

- Beat the eggs in a large bowl with the goat cheese. Add about ½ teaspoon salt and pepper to taste, and stir in the zucchini and the dill.

- Clean and dry the pan, and set it over medium-high heat. Heat the remaining tablespoon of olive oil in the skillet. Hold your hand above it; it should feel hot. Drop a bit of egg into the pan, and if it sizzles and cooks at once, the pan is ready. Pour in the egg and zucchini mixture. Swirl the pan to distribute the eggs and filling evenly over the surface. Shake the pan gently, tilting it slightly while lifting up the edges of the frittata with a spatula, to let the eggs run underneath during the first few minutes of cooking.

- Turn the heat down to low, cover, and cook 10 minutes, shaking the pan gently every once in a while. From time to time, remove the lid and loosen the bottom of the frittata with a wooden or rubber spatula, tilting the pan so the bottom doesn't burn. It will, however, turn golden. The eggs should be just about set.

• Meanwhile, heat the broiler. Uncover the pan and place under the broiler, not too close to the heat, for 1 to 3 minutes, until the top is set. Watch carefully to make sure the top doesn't burn (at most, it should brown very slightly and puff under the broiler). Remove from the heat, shake the pan to make sure the frittata isn't sticking, and let it cool for 5 to 15 minutes. Loosen the edges with a spatula. Carefully slide from the pan onto a large round platter. Cut into wedges or bite-size diamonds. Serve hot, warm, room temperature, or cold.

ADVANCE PREPARATION This can be made up to a day ahead if serving at room temperature.

Summer Squash Gratin

Makes 6 servings

2 to 2¼ pounds zucchini, or a mix of zucchini and yellow summer squash

3 tablespoons extra virgin olive oil

1 medium onion, peeled and chopped

2 to 3 large garlic cloves, minced, to taste

2 teaspoons fresh thyme leaves, or 1 teaspoon crumbled dried thyme

Salt and freshly ground black pepper

2 eggs

2 tablespoons minced flat-leaf parsley

1 cup cooked medium- or short-grain rice (such as arborio)

3 ounces Gruyère cheese, grated (¾ cup)

You can use just zucchini for this, or a mix of yellow and green squash. As in the frittatas, if you can cook the squash a day or several hours ahead and give it some time to drain, the texture of the gratin will be better because the liquid from the squash won't dilute the eggs and milk.

SPIRALIZING THE SQUASH Use the chipper (coarse shredder) blade. Take up handfuls of the spiralized squash and cut long strands into small pieces using scissors, or chop or cut in a food processor fitted with a steel blade.

● Preheat the oven to 375 degrees. Oil a 2-quart gratin dish.

● Heat 2 tablespoons of the olive oil in a large, heavy nonstick skillet over medium heat. Add the onion and cook, stirring often, until translucent, about 5 minutes. Add the garlic, stir together for about 30 seconds, until it begins to smell fragrant, and stir in the spiralized squash and the thyme. Cook, stirring often, until the squash is translucent but not mushy, about 5 minutes. Season generously with salt and pepper. If working ahead, place in a strainer set over a bowl, and let drain in the refrigerator for several hours or overnight.

● Beat the eggs in a large bowl. Beat in ½ teaspoon salt, stir in the parsley and rice, and add the cheese. Stir in the zucchini mixture and combine well. Scrape into the gratin dish. Drizzle the remaining tablespoon of olive oil over the top. Bake 40 to 45 minutes, or until the top is browned and the gratin is sizzling. Remove from the heat and let stand for at least 10 minutes before serving. Serve hot, warm, or at room temperature.

ADVANCE PREPARATION The gratin will keep, fully cooked, for 4 days in the refrigerator. Reheat in a medium-low oven.

Butternut Squash Gratin

Makes 4 to 6 servings

1 large butternut squash with a
  long neck
3 tablespoons extra virgin
  olive oil
  Salt and freshly ground black
  pepper
1 small onion, peeled and finely
  chopped
2 garlic cloves, minced
1 tablespoon finely chopped
  fresh sage
2 eggs
¾ cup milk
1 cup cooked medium-grain rice
  (such as arborio)
2 to 3 ounces Gruyère cheese,
  grated (½ to ¾ cup, tightly
  packed)

This Mediterranean gratin is adapted from a Provençal classic. The squash is spiralized on the thicker shredder blade, then cut into smaller pieces and roasted. The shreds look beautiful in the gratin, which is a mix of rice, Gruyère, onion, garlic, and sage, all held together with a couple of eggs beaten with a small amount of milk.

SPIRALIZING THE BUTTERNUT SQUASH Peel the squash and cut the long neck away from the round bulbous part. Spiralize the long neck using the chipper (coarse shredder) blade. Take up handfuls of the spiralized squash and cut long strands into 2-inch lengths with scissors. Seed the bottom half and cut into ½-inch pieces.

• Preheat the oven to 375 degrees. Cover a baking sheet with parchment. Toss the spiralized squash with 1 tablespoon of the olive oil and season with salt and pepper. Spread on the baking sheet in an even layer. Roast for 20 minutes, stirring halfway through, or until tender and caramelized.

• Oil a 2-quart baking dish with olive oil. Heat 1 tablespoon olive oil over medium heat in a medium-size skillet and add the onion. Cook, stirring often, until tender, about 5 minutes. Add a generous pinch of salt, the garlic, and the sage, and continue to cook, stirring, for another minute, until fragrant. Remove from the heat.

• Beat the eggs in a bowl. Beat in the milk and ½ teaspoon salt. Stir in the rice, onion mixture, the roasted squash, freshly ground pepper to taste, and the cheese. Combine thoroughly. Transfer to the prepared baking dish, and scrape out every last bit of filling with a rubber spatula. Drizzle the remaining 1 tablespoon olive oil over the top.

• Bake 35 to 45 minutes, until the sides are browned, the top is browned in places, and the gratin is sizzling. Remove from the oven and let stand for 10 minutes or longer before serving.

ADVANCE PREPARATION The roasted squash will keep for 2 to 3 days in the refrigerator. The finished gratin will also keep for 2 to 3 days. It's good at room temperature, or you can reheat it.

Cabbage, Potato, and Kale Gratin

Makes 6 servings

1 russet potato, peeled and trimmed

4 cups shredded savoy or green cabbage (½ medium head)

1 medium red or yellow onion, peeled

4 cups black kale leaves (also known as Tuscan kale or cavolo nero; 1 large bunch, stemmed, or use half of a 10-ounce bag)

3 tablespoons extra virgin olive oil

2 large garlic cloves, minced or pressed

2 teaspoons minced fresh sage (about 6 leaves)

Salt and freshly ground black pepper

3 eggs

¾ cup milk

3 tablespoons finely chopped flat-leaf parsley

2 ounces Gruyère cheese, grated (½ cup, tightly packed)

1 ounce Parmesan, grated (¼ cup)

Some people use the spiralizer to shred cabbage. I'm not sure if this goes faster than shredding it by hand, but you do get small shreds that cook down quickly. The cabbage, potatoes, and kale make a great combination. The cabbage sweetens as it cooks, the flavor and the color contrasting nicely with the dark green kale. Potatoes add bulk and comfort to this vegetarian dish.

SPIRALIZING THE POTATO Use the chipper (coarse shredder) blade. Cut ½ inch down the side of the potato to get half-moons, or take up handfuls and cut long strands of spiralized potato into 2-inch lengths with scissors.

SPIRALIZING THE CABBAGE (Optional) Use the chipper (coarse shredder) blade. Quarter and run the cabbage through the spiralizer. Alternatively, shred by hand.

SPIRALIZING THE ONION Use the shredder blade. Take up handfuls and cut long strands into 2-inch lengths with scissors.

• Bring a large pot of water to a boil, salt generously, and add the kale leaves. Blanch 3 minutes, until just tender. Transfer to a bowl of cold water and drain. Take up handfuls and squeeze out water. Cut each handful of kale crosswise into thin strips with scissors. Set aside.

• Bring the water back to a boil and add the spiralized potato. Turn the heat to medium and boil gently for 5 minutes. Drain and set aside.

• Preheat the oven to 375 degrees. Oil a 2-quart gratin or baking dish. Heat 2 tablespoons olive oil in a large heavy nonstick skillet over medium heat and add the onion. Cook, stirring often, until tender and translucent, 3 to 5 minutes. Stir in the garlic and cook, stirring until fragrant, about 30 seconds, then stir in the cabbage, sage, and salt to taste. Cook, stirring, until the cabbage is tender and fragrant, about 8 minutes. Stir in the kale and cook for another minute. Add pepper, taste, and adjust salt.

• Beat the eggs in a bowl. Whisk in the milk and ½ teaspoon salt, and stir in the potatoes, the cabbage and kale mixture, the parsley, Gruyère, and half the Parmesan. Stir together and scrape into the baking dish. Sprinkle the remaining Parmesan on top, and drizzle with remaining 1 tablespoon olive oil. Bake 30 to 40 minutes, until firm and browned on top. Serve hot or warm.

ADVANCE PREPARATION This can be made a day ahead and reheated. Or prepare the vegetables through Step 3 a day ahead, and assemble the gratin the next day. It will keep for 4 to 5 days in the refrigerator.

Southwestern Gratin with Zucchini, Red Peppers, and Corn

Makes 6 servings

¾ pound zucchini

1 large red bell pepper

1 medium onion

Kernels from 2 ears sweet corn (about 2 cups)

2 tablespoons extra virgin olive oil

Salt

1 large garlic clove, minced

Freshly ground black pepper

3 large eggs

¾ cup milk

1 teaspoon cumin seeds, lightly toasted and coarsely ground in a spice mill, or slightly crushed in a mortar and pestle

3 ounces Gruyère cheese, grates (¾ cup tightly packed)

This recipe works best if you can cook the vegetables a day ahead so they can drain overnight. The juices won't dilute the egg-and-milk custard, and the texture of the gratin will be creamier.

SPIRALIZING THE ZUCCHINI Use the slicer or the chipper (coarse shredder) blade. Cut into 2-inch lengths with scissors. Alternatively, make a ½-inch incision down the side of the zucchini before spiralizing.

SPIRALIZING THE RED PEPPER Use the shredder blade. Insert the bottom end into the spiralizer tube, and spiralize until you reach the seed pod. Cut away the flesh from the seed pod with a knife, and cut crosswise with scissors into thin strips. Cut long strands into 2-inch lengths with scissors.

SPIRALIZING THE ONION Use the chipper (coarse shredder) blade.

• Preheat the oven to 375 degrees. Oil a 2-quart gratin or baking dish. Set aside the kernels from one of the ears of corn. Heat the olive oil in a large skillet over medium heat and add the spiralized onion. Cook, stirring often, until it begins to soften, about 3 minutes, and add the spiralized red pepper and a generous pinch of salt. Cook, stirring often, until the onion and pepper are tender, about 5 minutes.

• Add the garlic and the spiralized zucchini, stir together, and add another generous pinch of salt and some pepper. Cook, stirring often, until the zucchini is just beginning to look bright green and some of the slices are translucent. Stir in the kernels from one of the ears of corn. Stir together for 1 to 2 minutes, and remove from the heat. Taste and adjust seasoning. Scrape into a colander set over a bowl. Let stand for an hour or, if possible, refrigerate uncovered overnight; drain liquid from the bowl.

• Place the remaining corn kernels in a blender and add the eggs, milk, and ½ teaspoon salt. Blend until smooth. Pour into the bowl with the vegetables. Add the cumin and the cheese and stir together. Scrape into the gratin dish.

• Bake 35 to 40 minutes, until the top is browned and the gratin is firm to the touch. Serve warm.

ADVANCE PREPARATION The vegetable filling can be prepared up to three days ahead and kept in the refrigerator.

Green Chilaquiles with Eggs and Zucchini

Makes 6 servings

1 pound zucchini (2 large)

2 tablespoons extra virgin olive oil or grapeseed oil

Salt

1½ pounds fresh tomatillos, husked and rinsed

2 to 4 jalapeño or serrano chiles, stemmed, to taste (seeded for a milder salsa)

12 cilantro sprigs, plus ⅓ cup chopped cilantro

1 small white onion, peeled, quartered, and thinly sliced (about 1 cup sliced onion) or spiralized on the shredder blade

2 large garlic cloves, minced

2 cups chicken or vegetable broth

6 large eggs

12 thick corn tortillas, cut into wedges and deep-fried or microwaved until crisp, or ½ pound thick tortilla chips from a Mexican grocery

½ cup crumbled queso fresco or feta

Chilaquiles is a comforting casserole that is made by combining a robust salsa or pureed beans with crispy tortillas. The dish can be more substantial with eggs or chicken, or as it is here, with vegetables. It makes a hearty breakfast but I serve it just as often for dinner.

SPIRALIZING THE ZUCCHINI Use the shredder blade. Take up handfuls of the spiralized zucchini and cut into 2-inch lengths with scissors.

● Heat 1 tablespoon oil over medium heat in a large, wide straight-sided skillet, and add the spiralized zucchini. Cook, stirring often, for about 3 minutes, just until tender. Season with salt and transfer to a strainer set over a bowl. Let stand for 1 hour, or preferably overnight in the refrigerator.

● Heat the broiler. Place the tomatillos and chiles on a baking sheet, and set about 4 inches below the broiler. Roast until dark and blackened in spots, about 5 minutes. Flip over and roast on other side until the tomatillos are soft and charred in spots, and the chiles are soft all the way through, 4 to 5 minutes. Remove from the heat and let cool for 5 minutes.

● Transfer the tomatillos, chiles, and cilantro sprigs to a blender, along with any juices that remain on the baking sheet. Blend to a coarse puree.

● Heat the remaining oil over medium heat in the skillet, and add the onion. Cook, stirring often, until tender, 5 to 8 minutes. Add a little salt, stir in the garlic, and cook, stirring, until fragrant, 30 seconds to 1 minute.

● Turn the heat to medium-high and add the tomatillo puree. Cook, stirring often, until the salsa thickens. Add the broth, bring to a simmer, and simmer 10 minutes or until the salsa coats the back of a spoon. Stir in the zucchini and heat through.

● Shortly before serving, beat the eggs in a bowl and season with salt to taste. Turn the heat to low, and stir the eggs into the salsa. Add the chopped cilantro, and stir until the eggs are set. The mixture should be creamy.

● Stir in the tortilla chips, making sure they are completely covered, and remove from heat. Sprinkle with crumbled cheese and serve at once.

Tortilla Española

Makes 6 servings

1 medium onion, peeled

3 medium Yukon gold potatoes (about 1½ pounds), peeled

4 tablespoons extra virgin olive oil

Salt and freshly ground black pepper

6 eggs

In the classic version of this popular Spanish tapa, the potatoes are sliced and the onions chopped, and the two are cooked together in abundant olive oil. You can use the slicer blade of your spiralizer to slice potatoes thin, but my first choice is the shredder blade. Instead of cooking the onions and potatoes together, which in my experience can result in burned onions, I cook the onions first, remove them from the pan, then cook the potatoes. A heavy nonstick pan works best for this.

SPIRALIZING THE ONION Use the shredder blade. Insert the onion into the spiralizer blade at the root end. Take up handfuls and cut into 2- to 3-inch lengths with scissors.

SPIRALIZING THE POTATOES Use the shredder blade. Take up handfuls and cut into 2- to 3-inch lengths.

- Heat 1 tablespoon of the olive oil over medium heat in a heavy 9- or 10-inch skillet. Add the onion and cook, stirring, until tender but not browned, 5 to 10 minutes. If it begins to stick and brown too much before it is tender, add a generous pinch of salt. Remove from the pan and transfer to a bowl. Add another 2 tablespoons of oil to the pan, and when hot, add the potatoes. Cook, stirring, until tender, 10 to 15 minutes. Stir in the onions, stir together and season generously with salt and pepper. Remove from the pan and transfer to a bowl to cool slightly.

- Beat the eggs in a bowl and add about ½ teaspoon salt and a generous amount of freshly ground pepper. Stir in the potatoes and onions.

- Heat the remaining olive oil over medium-high heat in the skillet. Hold your hand above it; it should feel hot. Drop a bit of egg into the pan, and if it sizzles and cooks at once, the pan is ready. Pour in the egg mixture. Swirl the pan to distribute the eggs and filling evenly over the surface. Shake the pan gently, tilting it slightly while lifting up the edges of the frittata with the spatula to let the eggs run underneath during the first few minutes of cooking.

- Turn the heat down to low, cover, and cook 10 minutes. From time to time remove the lid and loosen the bottom of the frittata with a wooden or rubber spatula, tilting the pan so the bottom doesn't burn. It will, however, turn a deep golden brown. The eggs should be just about set; cook a few minutes longer if they're not. Meanwhile, light the broiler.

● Finish the frittata under the broiler for 1 to 3 minutes, watching very carefully to make sure the top doesn't burn (at most, it should brown very slightly, and it will puff under the broiler). Remove from the heat, shake the pan to make sure the frittata isn't sticking, and let cool for 5 to 15 minutes. Loosen the edges with a wooden or rubber spatula. Carefully slide from the pan onto a large round platter. Cut into wedges or into bite-size diamonds. Serve warm, at room temperature, or cold.

ADVANCE PREPARATION The frittata can be made up to a day ahead of serving. Keep in the refrigerator, and bring to room temperature before serving.

Pipérade

Makes 6 servings

1 medium onion

2 large red bell peppers

1 large green bell pepper

2 tablespoons extra virgin
olive oil

2 large garlic cloves, minced

1 Anaheim pepper, cut into thin
2-inch-long slices

Salt

1 pound tomatoes, grated or
peeled, seeded, and chopped,
or 1 (14-ounce) can, drained
and chopped

Pinch of sugar

1 teaspoon fresh thyme leaves or
½ teaspoon dried thyme

Freshly ground black pepper to
taste

6 eggs

Pipérade is a Basque dish made with a variety of peppers. The word refers to pepper ragout, but it is also used for this egg dish, which is a comforting mix of the pepper ragout and scrambled eggs (and in the traditional dish, Bayonne ham). I use the spiralizer to get fine strips of peppers and onions.

SPIRALIZING THE ONION Use the shredder blade. Peel the onion and insert the root end into the spiralizer tube. Take up handfuls of spiralized onion and cut the long strands into 2-inch lengths with scissors.

SPIRALIZING THE PEPPERS Use the shredder blade. Insert the bottom end into the spiralizer tube, and spiralize until you reach the seed pod. Cut into 2-inch lengths with scissors. Cut away the flesh from the seed pod with a knife, and cut crosswise with scissors into thin strips. You won't be able to use the spiralizer for the Anaheim, which is too narrow.

● Heat the oil in a large heavy skillet or casserole over medium heat and add the spiralized onion. Cook, stirring, until tender, about 5 minutes, and add the garlic and peppers. Cook, stirring often, for 5 minutes, and add salt to taste. Continue to cook for another 5 minutes, until the peppers are tender.

● Add the tomatoes, sugar, thyme, and more salt and pepper to taste. Bring to a simmer. Cook, stirring from time to time, until the tomatoes have cooked down somewhat, about 10 minutes. Cover, reduce the heat, and simmer over low heat for another 15 to 20 minutes (or longer), stirring from time to time, until the mixture is thick and fragrant. It should not be watery at all. Taste and adjust seasoning.

● Beat the eggs in a bowl, season with salt and pepper, and stir into the peppers in the skillet. Cook, stirring over low heat, until the eggs are set. Remove from the heat and serve.

ADVANCE PREPARATION The stewed peppers will keep for about 5 days in the refrigerator.

Stewed Zucchini and Tomatoes with Eggs

Makes 6 servings

2 pounds zucchini, or a combination of green and yellow summer squash

1 medium onion, peeled

2 tablespoons extra virgin olive oil

4 garlic cloves, minced

Salt

2 pounds tomatoes, peeled, seeded and chopped (see Note), or 1 (28-ounce) can, drained and chopped

¼ teaspoon sugar

Freshly ground black pepper

6 eggs

NOTE When you seed the tomatoes, set a strainer over a bowl. Squeeze out the seeds into the strainer, then press the pulp and juice through the strainer into the bowl. Discard the seeds and use the juice in the recipe.

This is based on pisto, a comforting Spanish summer squash and tomato stew. In this spiralized version, the summer squash is not cooked down for as long as it would be in Spain, so the pieces stay intact. You can also serve the cooked vegetables without the eggs as a side dish.

SPIRALIZING THE SUMMER SQUASH Use the chipper (coarse shredder) blade. Take up handfuls and cut the long strands into 2-inch lengths with scissors.

SPIRALIZING THE ONION Use the shredder blade. Take up handfuls and cut the long strands into 2-inch lengths with scissors.

- Heat the oil over medium heat in a wide, heavy skillet and add the spiralized onion. Cook, stirring often, until just about tender, about 5 minutes. Add the garlic and cook, stirring, for 1 to 2 minutes, or until fragrant.

- Stir in the spiralized squash and about ½ teaspoon salt, and toss together for about 5 minutes, until the squash is coated with oil and beginning to soften. Add the tomatoes and their juice, the sugar, and salt to taste (½ to 1 teaspoon), and turn the heat to medium-high. Cook, stirring often, for 5 to 10 minutes, until the tomatoes have cooked down slightly. Turn the heat down to medium-low and cook uncovered, stirring often, for 15 minutes, until the vegetables are very tender. Taste, adjust the salt, and add lots of pepper.

- Using the back of your spoon, make six wells in the vegetable mixture and break an egg into each well. Sprinkle with salt and pepper. Cover the pan and cook until the eggs have set, about 6 to 8 minutes (the whites should be set but the yolks should still be runny).

ADVANCE PREPARATION The vegetable mixture will be delicious for 3 to 4 days, but don't cook the eggs until you reheat it.

Potato and Carrot Kugel

Makes 4 to 6 servings

1 pound Yukon gold or russet
potatoes, peeled and trimmed

½ pound fat carrots

½ medium onion, peeled

1 tablespoon butter

Salt

Freshly ground black pepper

2 tablespoons extra virgin
olive oil

½ cup low-fat cottage cheese

3 eggs

1 scant teaspoon caraway seeds,
lightly crushed

½ cup cooked black quinoa

A kugel is a sort of pudding, though mine are really more like gratins. Kugels can be sweet or savory, served as a side dish or a main. In this kugel, a mix of spiralized potatoes and carrots is speckled with black quinoa, a beautiful combination.

SPIRALIZING THE POTATOES Use the chipper (coarse shredder) blade. Take up handfuls of spiralized potatoes and cut the long strands into 2-inch lengths with scissors.

SPIRALIZING THE CARROTS Peel and cut away tapered end. Spiralize with the shredder blade. Take up handfuls of spiralized carrot and cut the long strands into 2-inch lengths with scissors.

SPIRALIZING THE ONION Use the shredder blade. Take up handfuls and cut into 2-inch lengths with scissors.

• Steam the spiralized potatoes above 1 inch boiling water for 5 minutes, until just tender. Transfer to a bowl, toss with the butter, season with salt and pepper, and set aside.

• Heat 1 tablespoon of the olive oil in a medium saucepan and add the spiralized onion. Cook, stirring, until just about tender, 3 to 5 minutes. Add the spiralized carrots and salt and pepper to taste. Cook, stirring, for another 3 minutes, until the carrots are just tender. Remove from the heat.

• Preheat the oven to 375 degrees. Oil a 2-quart baking dish or gratin dish.

• Combine the cottage cheese and eggs in a food processor fitted with the steel blade. Add ½ teaspoon salt, the caraway seeds, and a little pepper, and puree until smooth. Scrape into a large mixing bowl. Add the quinoa, potatoes, onions, and carrots, and mix together thoroughly. Scrape into the oiled baking dish. Drizzle the remaining oil over the top and place in the oven.

• Bake 35 to 40 minutes, until the top is lightly browned. Remove from the oven and let cool for at least 15 minutes before serving. Serve warm or room temperature, cut into squares or wedges.

ADVANCE PREPARATION The kugel will keep for 3 days in the refrigerator. Reheat in a medium oven.

Sweet Potato and Apple Kugel

Makes 8 servings

2 large sweet potatoes (1¾ to 2 pounds total), peeled and trimmed

2 tart apples, such as a Granny Smith or Braeburn, peeled

1 tablespoon fresh lime juice

Salt

4 eggs

½ cup crème fraîche

¼ cup mild honey or agave nectar

3 to 4 tablespoons melted unsalted butter, as needed

This sweet/tart combination makes a great Thanksgiving dish, though I will eat it any time of year. I cook the spiralized sweet potatoes briefly in boiling water before I bake the dish so that they soften sufficiently.

SPIRALIZING THE SWEET POTATOES Use the shredder blade. Take up handfuls of the spiralized sweet potato and cut into 2-inch lengths with scissors.

SPIRALIZING THE APPLES Use the shredder blade. Take up handfuls of the spiralized apple and cut into 2-inch lengths with scissors.

● Toss the spiralized apples with the lime juice. Preheat the oven to 375 degrees. Butter a 2-quart baking dish.

● Bring a pot of water to a boil, salt generously, and add the spiralized sweet potatoes. Boil 3 to 5 minutes, until just tender, and drain.

● In a large mixing bowl beat the eggs with the crème fraîche, ½ teaspoon salt, and the honey or agave nectar. Stir in 1 tablespoon melted butter. Add the sweet potatoes and apples. Combine well.

● Transfer the mixture to the prepared baking dish. Drizzle another tablespoon of the melted butter over the top. Bake 45 minutes.

● Turn the oven down to 350 degrees. Brush the top of the kugel with melted butter. Return to the oven and bake for another 20 minutes, or until the edges are browned, the top is browned in spots, and the mixture is set. Remove from the heat and let cool for 10 to 15 minutes before serving.

ADVANCE PREPARATION You can make this up to 3 days ahead and reheat in a medium oven.

Pasta

The popularity of the spiralizer began with spiralized vegetable pasta. Decades before this tool came along, many a chef and home cook spent hours making zucchini ribbons with a vegetable peeler or a mandoline. But the spiralizer has made it possible for the home cook to achieve vegetable noodles with such ease in preparation, it's no surprise that we've now begun to experiment with a range of produce.

Zucchini and summer squash in general remain the most popular vegetable noodles. I think it's because if the spiralized zucchini is cooked for no longer than 1½ minutes, the texture is similar to al dente pasta: slightly firm to the bite and slippery.

Summer squash noodles, because of the vegetable's high water content, will release water once they are cooked. This is not a problem as long as the water you cook the noodles in is salted, as it will assure a moist dish. I avoid thin sauces with zucchini noodles and focus on vegetable accompaniments. Other vegetable noodles, such as celeriac and rutabaga, will not be watery once cooked.

One of the most exciting discoveries that I made when working on this chapter was how wonderful beets are as a substitute for lasagna noodles (page 108). I steam the thin slices, spiralized on the slicing blade, until tender, then layer them in place of noodles with béchamel, greens, and Parmesan for a very convincing lasagna. Yellow beets work especially well because of the pale color.

No matter what vegetables you choose for your spiralized pasta, they will look beautiful against whatever sauce or vegetable accompaniment you choose. And the flavor, some say, is more exciting than wheat-based pasta. One thing is for sure: A spiralized pasta dinner will provide you with more vegetables than you may have ever dreamed you could eat at one sitting.

Zucchini Pasta with Ricotta and Peas

Makes 4 servings

2 to 2½ pounds zucchini
Salt
1½ cups shelled peas (about
    1¾ pounds in the pod)
1 garlic clove, mashed with a
    pinch of salt in a mortar and
    pestle
½ cup fresh ricotta cheese
2 tablespoons minced chives, or
    mixed herbs such as parsley,
    chives, and tarragon
    Freshly ground black pepper
1 tablespoon extra virgin olive oil
1 ounce Parmesan, grated
    (¼ cup tightly packed)

This is an easy, light springtime pasta. When I use ricotta in regular pasta dishes, I need to thin it out with pasta water. But zucchini noodles will provide enough liquid after you take them from the boiling water, so no additional liquid is needed.

SPIRALIZING THE ZUCCHINI Make a ½-inch slice down one side of the zucchini. Spiralize with the shredder blade to obtain curved pieces.

● Bring a large pot of water to a boil and salt generously. Add the peas and cook 4 to 5 minutes.

● Meanwhile, mix together the garlic and ricotta in a large bowl. Add the peas and stir in the herbs and pepper.

● Bring the water in the pot back to a boil and add the spiralized zucchini. Cook 1½ minutes, drain, and toss with the ricotta mixture, the olive oil, and the Parmesan. Taste, adjust seasoning, and serve.

ADVANCE PREPARATION You can make this through Step 2 a few hours ahead.

Zucchini Pasta with Pesto and Green Beans

Makes 4 servings

FOR THE PESTO

2 cups tightly packed, fresh basil leaves (about 1½ ounces)
Salt

2 tablespoons lightly toasted pine nuts or chopped walnuts (not toasted)

⅓ cup extra virgin olive oil

1½ to 2 ounces Parmesan, grated (⅓ to ½ cup tightly packed)

2 garlic cloves, halved, green shoots removed

FOR THE ZUCCHINI PASTA AND BEANS

2 to 2½ pounds zucchini

½ pound green beans or romano beans, trimmed and cut into 2-inch lengths

NOTE If making pesto and not making the pasta at the same time, you can blanch the basil in a smaller pot of boiling water.

One foolproof way you can make zucchini pasta taste rich is to coat it with pesto. When I make pesto, my first step is to blanch the basil leaves for 5 seconds. This ensures a bright green pesto that won't turn dark. It looks beautiful with the spiralized zucchini pasta and green beans.

SPIRALIZING THE ZUCCHINI Use the shredder blade. Take up handfuls of the spiralized zucchini and cut into manageable lengths with scissors.

• To make the pesto, bring a large pot of water to a boil while you rinse the basil leaves (you'll also use this water for cooking the green beans and the zucchini pasta). Fill a bowl with ice water, and place it next to the saucepan with a skimmer close by (a Chinese skimmer is good for this). When the water comes to a boil, salt generously and add the basil leaves. Push them down into the water with the back of the skimmer to submerge, count to five, then remove immediately with the skimmer and transfer to the ice water. Drain and squeeze out excess water.

• Place the pine nuts or walnuts in a food processor and process until finely ground. Add the blanched basil and salt to taste (I use ¼ to ½ teaspoon kosher salt), and process until finely chopped. With the machine running, slowly add the olive oil and continue to process for a full minute, or until the mixture is reduced to a fine puree. Transfer to a bowl. Alternatively, place all of the ingredients for the pesto except the cheese and garlic into the jar that comes with an immersion blender, and blend with the immersion blender until smooth.

• When you are ready to use the pesto, puree the garlic in a mortar and pestle, or put through a garlic press, and stir into the pesto (or if using a mortar and pestle, add the pureed basil and garlic together to the mortar and work the garlic and pesto together). Add the cheese and stir in. The pesto will compress when you add the cheese, so even though you've added ½ cup cheese to the puree, you will end up with about ⅔ cup pesto.

- Bring the water in the pot back to a boil and add the green beans. Blanch for 5 minutes, remove with the skimmer, and transfer to a bowl of cold water. Drain.

- Place half the pesto in a large, wide bowl for the pasta. Add a tablespoon of the cooking water to the remaining pesto, and place in a bowl to pass at the table. Bring the water in the pot back to a boil and add the zucchini noodles. Cook 1½ minutes and drain. Transfer to the bowl, and toss with the green beans and pesto. Serve at once, passing additional pesto and Parmesan at the table.

ADVANCE PREPARATION The pesto will keep for a week in the refrigerator, but it tastes best if you wait until you plan to use it before adding the garlic and cheese. It freezes well, without the garlic and cheese added.

VARIATION **Basil-Mint Pesto**

- Substitute ½ cup fresh mint leaves for ½ cup of the basil. Proceed with the pesto recipe as directed.

Zucchini Fusilli with Tomatoes, Arugula, and Feta

Makes 4 servings

2 to 2½ pounds zucchini

1 box cherry tomatoes, halved or quartered

1 plump garlic clove, minced (more to taste)

Salt

1 teaspoon balsamic vinegar

1 cup chopped arugula

1 tablespoon slivered or chopped fresh basil

2 tablespoons extra virgin olive oil

2 ounces feta or goat cheese, crumbled (½ cup)

This is a perfect summer meal that couldn't be easier to throw together. The tomato and arugula accompaniment is uncooked, so this is as much a salad as a pasta dish. Try to find wild arugula—the feathery, more pungent variety—and the sweetest cherry tomatoes you can get.

SPIRALIZING THE ZUCCHINI Use the slicer blade. Take up handfuls of the spiralized zucchini and cut long strands into 3-inch lengths with scissors.

● Combine the cherry tomatoes, garlic, salt to taste, balsamic vinegar, arugula, basil, and olive oil in a wide bowl. Let stand for 15 minutes. Taste and adjust seasonings.

● Meanwhile, bring a large pot of water to a rolling boil. Salt generously and add the spiralized zucchini. Cook 1 to 1½ minutes, drain and toss with the tomato mixture. Sprinkle on the cheese and serve.

ADVANCE PREPARATION You can assemble the tomato and arugula mixture a few hours ahead.

Zucchini Fusilli with Asparagus, Fava Beans, Green Garlic, and Herbs

Makes 4 servings

2 to 2½ pounds zucchini

2 pounds fava beans, shelled

1 pound asparagus, preferably fat stalks

Salt

2 tablespoons extra virgin olive oil

1 bulb green garlic, papery shells discarded, minced

1 tablespoon minced fresh chives

2 tablespoons chopped flat-leaf parsley or marjoram

Freshly ground black pepper

Freshly grated Parmesan

This is a heavenly springtime pasta. Use fat stalks of asparagus if you can find them for the most luxurious results. Fava beans take a while to shell and skin, but the effort will be worth it.

SPIRALIZING THE ZUCCHINI Use the slicer blade. Take up handfuls of the spiralized zucchini and cut long strands into 3-inch lengths with scissors.

- Begin heating a large pot of water while you shell the favas. Fill a bowl with cold water. When the water comes to a boil, salt generously and add the beans. Boil small beans for 2 to 3 minutes, larger beans for 4 to 5 minutes. Using a skimmer or a strainer, transfer the favas to the bowl of cold water. Allow the beans to cool for several minutes, then drain and slip off their skins by pinching off the eye of the skin and squeezing gently. Set aside in a bowl.

- Break off the tough stem ends from the asparagus and discard. Add the asparagus to the boiling water. Boil for 4 minutes, until just tender. Using the skimmer or strainer, scoop the asparagus out of the water, transfer to a bowl of cold water and drain. Pat dry and cut into 1-inch lengths. Add to the bowl with the fava beans.

- Drain the water from the pot and fill with fresh water. Bring to a boil and salt generously.

- Heat 1 tablespoon of the olive oil over medium heat in a large, heavy skillet and add the green garlic. Cook gently, stirring, until translucent, 1 to 2 minutes, and stir in the favas, asparagus, and herbs. If you are still waiting for the water to boil, take off the heat. Otherwise, keep warm.

- Add the spiralized zucchini to the salted boiling water. Cook 1½ minutes. Drain (or use tongs to remove from the water) and transfer to the skillet. Add the remaining olive oil, and salt and pepper to taste; toss together and serve. Pass the Parmesan at the table.

ADVANCE PREPARATION You can prepare the vegetables through Step 4 several hours before cooking the zucchini.

Celeriac or Zucchini Pasta with Baby Broccoli and Red Pepper Flakes

Makes 4 servings

2 pounds celeriac, or 2 to 2½ pounds zucchini

Salt

1 pound baby broccoli (broccolini), ends trimmed

3 tablespoons extra virgin olive oil

2 garlic cloves, minced

¼ to ½ teaspoon red pepper flakes

2 ounces ricotta salata, Parmesan, or a mix of pecorino and Parmesan, grated (½ cup tightly packed)

Broccoli makes a great "sauce" with spiralized pasta. Cook it until it is soft enough to fall apart when you chop it up, and it will blend beautifully with the pasta. My first choice for pasta here is celeriac. The flavor is perfect with the baby broccoli.

SPIRALIZING THE CELERIAC OR ZUCCHINI Use the shredder blade. Take up handfuls of the spiralized celeriac or zucchini and cut into manageable lengths with scissors.

- Bring a large pot of water to a boil. Salt generously and add the baby broccoli. Cook for 5 minutes, until tender, and transfer using a spider strainer or a skimmer to a bowl of cold water. Drain. Chop fine. Set aside the water for the spiralized vegetable.

- Heat the oil over medium heat in a heavy skillet, and add the garlic and red pepper flakes. Cook until the garlic smells fragrant, 30 seconds to a minute, and add the chopped baby broccoli. Toss together for a minute, season to taste with salt, and remove from the heat but keep warm.

- Bring the water back to a boil and add the spiralized celeriac or zucchini. Cook zucchini for 1½ minutes, celeriac for 1½ to 2 minutes. Drain and toss with the baby broccoli and cheese, either right in the skillet or in a warm bowl. Serve at once.

ADVANCE PREPARATION The broccoli can be prepared through Step 2 a day ahead and refrigerated. Reheat in a large skillet.

Pasta with Zucchini and Mint

Makes 4 servings

2 pounds celeriac, or 2 to 2½ pounds zucchini or yellow summer squash

1½ pounds zucchini, for the topping

2 tablespoons extra virgin olive oil

Salt and freshly ground black pepper

¼ teaspoon sugar

1 tablespoon plus 1 teaspoon sherry vinegar or lemon juice

1 teaspoon finely minced lemon zest

1 tablespoon chopped fresh mint

Freshly grated pecorino or Parmesan

Zucchini and mint make a wonderful pairing. I have made this with both celeriac and summer squash pasta, which might seem like a lot of zucchini for one meal, but nobody even minds.

SPIRALIZING THE CELERIAC, ZUCCHINI, OR YELLOW SUMMER SQUASH Use the shredder blade. Take up handfuls of the spiralized celeriac, zucchini, or yellow summer squash and cut into manageable lengths with scissors.

SPIRALIZING THE ZUCCHINI FOR THE TOPPING Use the slicer blade. Cut down one or two sides of the zucchini so that the zucchini will slice off in rings or half-moons.

● Bring a large pot of water to a boil for the spiralized pasta.

● Meanwhile, heat the oil over medium heat in a large, heavy nonstick skillet and add the sliced zucchini for the topping. Cook, stirring or shaking the pan, until the zucchini is tender, about 3 minutes. Season generously with salt and pepper, add the sugar, and stir in the vinegar or lemon juice, lemon zest, and mint. Remove from the heat and keep warm while you cook the pasta.

● When the pasta cooking water comes to a boil, salt generously and add the spiralized celeriac or squash noodles. Cook 1½ minutes. Drain and toss with the zucchini topping. Top each serving with grated pecorino or Parmesan.

ADVANCE PREPARATION Although this is best when served just after cooking, the zucchini topping could be cooked a few hours ahead. But don't add the vinegar or lemon juice or the mint until you heat through before serving.

Summer Squash Ribbons with Fresh Favas and Herbs

Makes 4 servings

2 to 2½ pounds yellow summer squash or zucchini, or a mix
Salt

2 pounds fava beans, shelled

2 tablespoons extra virgin olive oil

1 green garlic bulb, papery shells discarded, minced, or 2 large regular garlic cloves, minced

3 tablespoons chopped mixed herbs, such as chives, basil, parsley, tarragon, marjoram
Freshly ground black pepper

2 ounces feta, crumbled (½ cup)

A big bowl of green and yellow squash ribbons is a beautiful thing to behold. Even better, a big frying pan with the barely cooked ribbons tossed with bright favas, herbs, and feta.

SPIRALIZING THE SQUASH Use the slicer blade. Take up handfuls of the spiralized squash and cut into manageable lengths with scissors.

● Begin heating a large pot of water while you shell the favas. Fill a bowl with cold water. When the water comes to a boil, salt generously and add the favas. Boil small beans for 2 to 3 minutes, larger beans for 5 minutes. Using a skimmer or strainer, transfer the favas to the bowl of cold water. Allow the beans to cool for several minutes, then slip off their skins by pinching off the eye of the skin and squeezing gently. Set aside.

● Heat 1 tablespoon of the olive oil over medium-low heat in a large, heavy skillet and add the garlic. Cook gently, stirring, until translucent, 2 to 3 minutes for green garlic, 30 seconds to a minute for regular garlic. Stir in the favas and herbs.

● Bring the water in the pot back to a boil and add the squash ribbons. Cook 1 minute. Using a ladle, transfer ½ cup of the pasta cooking water to a small bowl, in case you want more to moisten the mixture. Drain the squash noodles, and add to the pan with the favas and herbs. Add the remaining olive oil, salt and pepper to taste, and the feta, and toss together using tongs. Add more of the cooking water, if desired (the summer squash continues to release water so you probably will not need more). Use tongs to serve.

ADVANCE PREPARATION You can prepare the vegetables through Step 2 several hours before cooking the squash noodles.

Beet Pasta with Beet Greens and Goat Cheese

Makes 4 servings

2 pounds beets, peeled and trimmed

3 tablespoons extra virgin olive oil

2 plump garlic cloves, minced or put through a press

½ to 1 teaspoon chopped fresh rosemary

½ to 1 teaspoon fresh thyme leaves, or ½ teaspoon dried thyme

1 pound stemmed beet greens or spinach, washed thoroughly twice and coarsely chopped (8 cups tightly packed)

Salt

Freshly ground black pepper

4 ounces soft goat cheese, crumbled (1 cup)

Red beets make beautiful noodles. I always buy beets by the bunch, with the greens still attached, and the abundance of the greens in the bunch is just as important to me as the size of the beets. If you can't find beets with the greens attached, substitute fresh spinach for the beet greens.

SPIRALIZING THE BEETS Use the shredder blade. Take up handfuls of the spiralized beets and cut long strands into manageable lengths with scissors.

- Bring 1 inch of water to a boil in a large steamer or pasta pot. Place the spiralized beets in the steamer or pasta basket, set over the water, cover tightly and steam for 10 minutes, until cooked al dente. The noodles should be cooked through and flexible but not mushy.

- Meanwhile, heat 2 tablespoons of the olive oil over medium-high heat in a wide, heavy skillet and add the garlic, rosemary, and thyme. Cook, stirring, until the garlic is fragrant, 30 seconds to a minute, and, a handful at a time, add the greens, which should still be wet from washing. As each handful begins to collapse, add another handful, and when all of the greens have been added, season with salt and cook, stirring, until wilted and tender, 3 to 5 minutes. Add pepper; taste and adjust seasoning.

- When the beet pasta is ready, transfer to a large bowl and toss with the remaining olive oil and salt to taste.

- Stir half the goat cheese into the wilted greens, and heat until the cheese has melted.

- Distribute the beet pasta among four plates, or pile onto a platter. Top with the greens. Sprinkle on the remaining goat cheese and serve.

ADVANCE PREPARATION The beet noodles can be cooked a few days ahead and reheated. The greens can be prepared through Step 2 up to 3 days ahead and refrigerated.

Golden Beet Lasagna

Makes 6 servings

1¾ pounds golden beets, with greens

Salt

1 tablespoon butter

2 tablespoons extra virgin olive oil (or omit butter and use 3 tablespoons olive oil)

3 tablespoons minced shallot or onion

3 tablespoons sifted all-purpose flour

3 cups milk

Freshly ground black pepper

Pinch of freshly grated nutmeg

4 ounces Parmesan cheese, grated (1 cup tightly packed)

¼ cup finely chopped fresh herbs, such as parsley, tarragon, dill, chives

NOTE If you can't find golden beets with the greens attached, substitute ½ pound Swiss chard. Stem and follow directions for the beet greens.

NOTE You may substitute a gluten-free all-purpose flour mix for the flour.

This got the vote in my house for best recipe in the book. It's a gorgeous, luxurious dish, a layered casserole with spiralized golden beets standing in for lasagna noodles. The beet greens are blanched and chopped fine, then stirred into the béchamel along with chopped fresh herbs. If you find very large golden beets at the farmers market, buy them and use them here; they are perfect for this. Close your eyes and you can almost imagine you are eating real pasta.

SPIRALIZING THE BEETS Use the slicer blade. Cut or break into rounds.

● Cut the greens away from the beets. Peel, trim, and spiralize the beets as directed. Stem and wash the greens well in two changes of water. Set aside.

● Place the spiralized beets in a steamer above 1 inch of boiling water. Steam 15 minutes, until tender. Remove the steamer basket from the pot and allow the beets to cool.

● Meanwhile, add more water to the steamer pot and bring to a boil. When the water comes to a boil, salt generously and add the greens. Blanch 1 to 2 minutes, until just tender. Transfer to a bowl of cold water, drain, and squeeze out excess water. Chop fine.

● Make the béchamel. In a heavy medium saucepan, heat the butter and oil over medium heat. Add the shallot or onion and cook, stirring, until softened, about 2 minutes. Stir in the flour and cook, stirring, for about 3 minutes, until smooth and bubbling but not browned; it should have the texture of wet sand. Whisk in the milk all at once and bring to a simmer, whisking. When the mixture begins to thicken, turn the heat to very low and simmer, stirring often with a whisk and scraping the bottom and edges of the pan with a rubber spatula, for 10 to 15 minutes, until the sauce is creamy and has lost its raw flour taste. Season with salt, pepper, and nutmeg. Strain while hot into a large measuring cup or a medium bowl, and stir in ¼ cup of the Parmesan, the chopped greens, and the herbs.

● Preheat the oven to 350 degrees. Oil a rectangular baking dish. Spread a small spoonful of béchamel over the bottom. Top with a layer of beets. Spoon a thin layer of the béchamel over the beets and sprinkle with Parmesan. Repeat the layers twice, ending with a layer of beets topped with béchamel and Parmesan. Make sure the beets are well coated with béchamel.

● Bake 30 to 40 minutes, until the top is browned and the mixture is bubbling. Remove from the oven and allow to stand for 5 to 10 minutes before serving.

Celeriac Pasta with Chickpeas and Marinara Sauce

Makes 4 servings

2 pounds celeriac (2 good-size bulbs), ends trimmed, peeled
Salt
1 cup Easy Marinara Sauce (recipe below)
1 tablespoon minced parsley or slivered basil
1 (15-ounce) can chickpeas, drained and rinsed, or 1½ cups cooked chickpeas
1 tablespoon extra virgin olive oil
Freshly grated Parmesan

FOR THE EASY MARINARA SAUCE

1 (28-ounce) can whole tomatoes
1 tablespoon extra virgin olive oil
2 cloves garlic, minced or thinly sliced
Pinch of sugar
Pinch of salt
Few sprigs of fresh basil
Slivered fresh basil leaves (optional)

Celeriac pasta may be my favorite of the spiralized vegetable pastas. The noodles are tasty, not watery, with some substance as long as you don't overcook them. If you have marinara sauce on hand, this is ready in minutes.

SPIRALIZING THE CELERIAC Use the shredder blade. Take up handfuls of spiralized celeriac and cut long strands into manageable lengths with scissors.

- Prepare the celeriac while you bring a large pot of water to a boil.

- Meanwhile, make the marinara sauce (or heat the marinara sauce you have on hand). In a food processor, pulse the tomatoes so that you have a nice puréed texture. Heat 1 tablespoon olive oil over medium heat in a wide nonstick skillet or saucepan. Add garlic, and as soon as it begins to smell fragrant (30 seconds to 1 minute), add the tomatoes, sugar, salt, and basil sprigs and turn up the heat. When the tomatoes begin to bubble, turn the heat to medium and cook, stirring often, until thick and fragrant, 20 to 30 minutes. Stir in slivered fresh basil, and, if desired, cook for another couple of minutes. Remove from the heat, taste and adjust seasoning.

- When ready to serve, salt the boiling water generously, add the celeriac noodles and boil 1½ minutes. Drain and toss with the marinara sauce, the parsley or basil, the chickpeas, and the olive oil. Serve at once, passing the Parmesan for sprinkling.

ADVANCE PREPARATION Marinara sauce keeps for 3 to 4 days in the refrigerator and freezes well. The celeriac can be spiralized up to 4 days ahead.

Celeriac Pasta with Green Beans, Black Pepper, and Goat Cheese

Makes 4 servings

2 pounds celeriac, trimmed and peeled

Salt

¾ pound green beans, ends trimmed

6 ounces goat cheese

½ to 1 teaspoon freshly ground black pepper

2 tablespoons minced flat-leaf parsley

2 tablespoons minced fresh chives

2 tablespoons extra virgin olive oil

Goat cheese makes a delicious pairing with celeriac and green beans. When you toss the celeriac pasta with the goat cheese, the cheese melts into a creamy sauce, resulting in a luxurious yet light meal.

SPIRALIZING THE CELERIAC Use the shredder blade. Take up handfuls and cut long strands into manageable lengths using scissors.

• Bring a large pot of water to a boil and salt generously. Fill a bowl with ice water. Add the beans to the pot and cook 5 minutes, until tender. Transfer to the ice water, then drain. Cut away the stem ends, and cut the beans into 2-inch lengths.

• Place the goat cheese in a large pasta bowl, and thin out with ¼ cup of the hot water from the pot.

• Bring the water back to a boil and add the celeriac. Cook 1½ minutes, add the beans back to the pot to heat through, then remove ¼ cup water and set aside. Drain the celeriac and green beans and toss with the diluted goat cheese. Add the pepper, parsley, chives, and olive oil. Toss together until the celeriac is coated with the cheese. If desired, thin out with some of the pasta water you set aside. Serve hot.

ADVANCE PREPARATION The spiralized celeriac will keep for up to 3 days in the refrigerator.

Rutabaga or Celeriac Pasta with Leeks and Kale

Makes 4 to 6 servings

2 pounds rutabaga or celeriac, peeled and trimmed

1 tablespoon unsalted butter

1 tablespoon extra virgin olive oil (or omit butter and use 2 tablespoons olive oil)

2 large leeks, white and light green parts only, cleaned, cut in half lengthwise, and sliced

4 fresh sage leaves, cut into thin slivers

Salt

¾ pound kale (1 generous bunch), stemmed, washed thoroughly, and cut crosswise in strips (about 5 cups)

Freshly ground black pepper

2 ounces Parmesan, grated (½ cup tightly packed)

2 ounces Fontina or Gruyère cheese, grated (½ cup tightly packed)

Rutabaga, that vegetable that looks like an oversize yellow turnip, has a perfect flavor for this dish, which is an adaptation of an Italian pasta recipe that also calls for cabbage. The rutabaga has a flavor that is mildly cruciferous, milder and sweeter than a turnip. The strands break up very quickly when you boil them, so you may get a pasta dish that is more like one made with fusilli or penne than long spaghetti strands. Celeriac also works well here.

SPIRALIZING THE RUTABAGA OR CELERIAC Use the shredder blade. Take up handfuls of the spiralized rutabaga or celeriac and cut long strands into manageable lengths using scissors.

• Begin heating a large pot of water. Meanwhile, heat the butter and oil in a large heavy skillet over medium-low heat. Add the leeks and sage, and cook, stirring often, until the leeks begin to soften, about 3 minutes. Add ½ teaspoon salt and continue to cook, stirring often, until the leeks are tender, about 3 minutes. Try to avoid letting the leeks brown too much. Remove from the heat.

• When the water comes to a boil, salt generously and add the kale. Boil for 4 minutes, until tender but still bright. Using a slotted spoon or a skimmer, transfer to the pan with the leeks and stir together. Season with salt and pepper to taste. Keep warm over low heat.

• When ready to serve, bring the water back to a boil and add the rutabaga or celeriac. Boil 1½ minutes; transfer, using a skimmer or pasta fork, to the pan with the kale and leeks. Toss in the pan or in a warm pasta bowl with the leeks, kale, and the cheeses. Serve at once.

ADVANCE PREPARATION You can make the dish through Step 2 and take off the heat several hours ahead. Reheat when you cook the pasta.

Fish, Meat, and Tacos

I've grouped together a variety of meat, fish, and seafood dishes in this chapter, as well as some vegetarian tacos. What all of the recipes have in common is an abundance of vegetables accompanying the animal proteins, as well as no shortage of big flavors.

Vegetables never take a back seat when I serve meat or fish. The two always go hand in hand, as in the chicken fajitas (page 126), where the seared spiralized peppers, onions, and squash that accompany the chicken are as important as the chicken itself (or the beef and shrimp in the variations). I serve Winter Squash Noodles with Miso-Glazed Salmon (page 120) and pay as much if not more attention to the vegetable slaw as I do to the chicken in my Chicken Tacos with Creamy Kohlrabi Slaw (page 133).

Stir-fries are perfect vehicles for spiralized noodles and for other vegetables that can be quickly prepared with the spiralizer, like the peppers and onions called for in Rainbow Beef (page 130). The spicy Malaysian zucchini noodles with shrimp (page 122) and the Stir-Fried Zucchini Noodles with Chicken and Peppers (page 125) have become mainstays in my house. The texture of stir-fried noodles, especially zucchini noodles, is addictive. This has opened up a wide range of possibilities for dinner when I have a small amount of meat or fish in the refrigerator and a lot of zucchini or other vegetables that can be turned into noodles in my vegetable bin.

Oven-Steamed Salmon
with Marinated Cucumbers

Makes 4 servings

1 large European cucumber or
2 large regular cucumbers
(1¼ to 1½ pounds), peeled if
desired

Salt

¼ cup seasoned rice wine vinegar

Pinch of hot red pepper flakes

1 tablespoon dark sesame oil

1 large (1½-pound) salmon fillet,
or 4 (6-ounce) fillets, skin on

Extra virgin olive oil

Freshly ground black pepper

I try to keep marinated spiralized cucumbers on hand in the refrigerator for salads and side dishes. This pretty, quick pickle in a sweet-and-sour rice vinegar brine with hot pepper flakes and nutty sesame oil is one of my favorites; it goes particularly well with salmon. Marinated cucumbers taste best to me when they are sliced exceptionally thin, as you can do with a spiralizer.

SPIRALIZING THE CUCUMBER Make a ½-inch incision one side of the cucumber. Use the slicer blade to cut thin rounds.

• Place the rounds of cucumber in a colander in the sink. Sprinkle generously with salt and allow to drain for 15 to 30 minutes.

• Drain the cucumbers on paper towels and toss with the seasoned vinegar, pepper flakes, and the sesame oil. Refrigerate while you cook the salmon.

• Preheat the oven to 300 degrees. Cover a baking sheet with foil and oil lightly. Place the salmon on top. Season with salt and gently rub the salt into the surface of the salmon. Add pepper to taste. Fill a roasting pan with boiling water and place it on the oven floor.

• Place the salmon in the oven and bake until the fish flakes and white bubbles of protein appear on the surface, 10 to 20 minutes, depending on the size of the fillets. Remove from the oven.

• Garnish each piece of salmon with the marinated cucumbers.

ADVANCE PREPARATION The marinated cucumbers will keep for 3 to 4 days in the refrigerator.

Winter Squash Noodles with Miso-Glazed Salmon and Leeks

Makes 4 servings

1 large or 2 medium butternut squash, with long necks (about 4 pounds)

Salt

¼ cup mirin

¼ cup sake

3 tablespoons white or yellow miso paste

1 tablespoon brown sugar

2 teaspoons dark sesame oil

4 salmon or arctic char fillets, about 6 ounces each, skin on if possible

4 tablespoons extra virgin olive oil

2 large leeks, white and light green parts only, cleaned thoroughly and sliced

Spiralized winter squash noodles will fall apart if you try to boil them, but you can toss them with oil and roast them in the oven with delicious results. You can roast them ahead and reheat for this easy weeknight dinner that is also special enough to serve for a dinner party.

SPIRALIZING THE BUTTERNUT SQUASH Peel the squash and cut the long neck away from the round bulbous part. Spiralize the long neck using the shredder blade. Take up handfuls of the spiralized squash and cut into manageable lengths with scissors.

● Combine the mirin and sake in the smallest saucepan you have and bring to a boil over high heat. Boil 20 seconds, taking care not to boil off much of the liquid, then turn the heat to low and stir in the miso and brown sugar. Whisk over medium heat until the sugar has dissolved. Remove from the heat and whisk in the sesame oil. Let cool. Transfer to a wide heatproof glass or ceramic baking dish.

● Pat the fish fillets dry and brush or rub on both sides with the marinade, then place them in the baking dish and turn them over a few times in the marinade remaining in the dish. Cover with plastic wrap and marinate for 2 to 3 hours, or up 12 hours.

● Preheat the oven to 375 degrees. Line two baking sheets with parchment. Divide the spiralized winter squash between the baking sheets and toss each batch with 1½ tablespoons of olive oil and salt to taste. Place in the oven and roast for 10 minutes. Stir the squash noodles or toss with tongs, and switch the baking sheets back to front and top to bottom if roasting on two levels. Roast for another 5 to 10 minutes, until the noodles are tender and beginning to color. Keep warm.

- Turn up the oven to 400 degrees.

- Remove the salmon from the refrigerator and transfer from the baking dish to a plate. Add 3 tablespoons water or sake to the marinade left in the baking dish, and add the leeks. Toss until thoroughly coated. Place in the oven and bake 15 to 20 minutes or until tender, stirring every 5 minutes. Remove from the heat and keep warm.

- Heat the remaining 1 tablespoon olive oil in a large heavy skillet over medium-high heat, or prepare a medium-hot grill. Place the fish skin side down in the pan or on the grill. Cook for 3 minutes on each side, until the surface browns and blackens in spots. If necessary (this will depend on the thickness of the fillets), finish in the oven for about 5 minutes, until the fish is opaque but still moist. Remove from the oven.

- Place a serving of butternut squash noodles on each plate. Top with a fish fillet, garnish with the leeks, and serve.

ADVANCE PREPARATION You can prepare the fish 12 hours before cooking. The noodles will keep for a couple of days in the refrigerator.

Malaysian-Style Zucchini Noodles with Greens and Shrimp

Makes 4 servings

2½ pounds zucchini

½ pound turnip greens or mustard greens, cleaned, thick stem ends discarded (about 8 cups leaves)

Salt

¾ pound green cabbage (½ medium head), quartered, cored and cut in ¾-inch dice (about 4½ cups)

2 tablespoons soy sauce

¾ teaspoon salt

2 teaspoons brown sugar

2 teaspoons cornstarch

1 tablespoon Asian red chile paste or sauce, such as sambal oelek

2 tablespoons grapeseed, peanut, or canola oil

2 large garlic cloves, minced

1 tablespoon minced fresh ginger

⅔ pound medium shrimp (about 24), shelled, cut in half lengthwise, and deveined

¼ cup cilantro

1 lime, cut into wedges

"That was the best dinner I've ever had," read the text from my sister after I tested this recipe, left her a dinner plate, and ran out the door, late for a meeting. The pungent mix of zucchini noodles, greens, cabbage, shrimp, and chile is indeed wonderful. Even the shrimp look spiralized since they curl when they hit the wok. My sister couldn't believe there were no noodles of any kind in the dish.

SPIRALIZING THE ZUCCHINI Use the shredder blade. Take up handfuls of the spiralized zucchini and cut long strands into manageable lengths with scissors.

● Bring a large pot of water to a boil, salt generously, and add the greens. Cook 30 seconds only and immediately transfer to a bowl of ice water, using a slotted spoon or deep-fry skimmer. Drain, squeeze out water, and chop coarsely. Set aside. Bring the water back to a boil, add the cabbage, blanch 30 seconds, and transfer to the ice water. Drain and set aside.

● Bring the water back to a boil and add the spiralized zucchini. Cook 1 minute, drain, shake off excess water, and set aside.

● In a small bowl mix together the soy sauce, salt, brown sugar, cornstarch, and chile paste. Stir to dissolve the sugar and salt, and set aside.

● Heat a wok or large heavy nonstick skillet over medium-high heat until a drop of water evaporates upon contact. Swirl in the oil and add the garlic and ginger. Cook, stirring, for about 15 seconds or until the garlic and ginger are fragrant. Add the shrimp and cook, stirring, until the shrimp curl and turn pink, about 2 minutes. Add the cabbage and greens and stir-fry another 2 minutes, until the cabbage is crisp-tender. Add the zucchini noodles and soy sauce mixture, and stir together until the noodles are heated through and coated with the sauce. Add the cilantro, toss together quickly, and remove from the heat. Serve with lime wedges on the side.

ADVANCE PREPARATION You can prep all the ingredients hours ahead. Keep in the refrigerator.

Stir-Fried Zucchini Noodles with Chicken and Peppers

Makes 4 servings

2 to 2½ pounds zucchini

1 large red pepper

1 large yellow pepper

Salt

2 tablespoons soy sauce or Thai fish sauce

2 teaspoons brown sugar

1 teaspoon cornstarch

1 tablespoon Asian red chile paste or sauce, such as sambal oelek

1 pound boneless, skinless chicken breast, cut across the grain into ¼-inch-thick slices

2 tablespoons grapeseed, peanut, or canola oil

2 large garlic cloves, minced

1 tablespoon minced fresh ginger

2 to 4 tablespoons chopped cilantro

Lime wedges

My world of stir-fried noodles expanded exponentially when I started spiralizing zucchini. This stir-fry is spiced up with chile sauce. I use sambal oelek, which I keep on hand in the refrigerator. The pale green noodles look beautiful against the red and yellow peppers and lightly browned chicken.

SPIRALIZING THE ZUCCHINI Use the shredder blade. Take up handfuls of the spiralized zucchini and cut long strands into manageable lengths.

SPIRALIZING THE PEPPERS Use the shredder blade. Insert the bottom end into the spiralizer tube and spiralize until you reach the seed pod. When you reach the seed pod, remove pepper from the spiralizer and cut the remaining flesh (about one-third of the pepper) away from the seeds. Slice crosswise the same thickness as the spiralized portion. Take up handfuls of the spiralized peppers and cut long strands into 2- to 3-inch lengths.

- Fill a medium-size saucepan with water and bring to a boil. Salt generously and add the zucchini noodles. Boil 1 minute. Transfer to a bowl of cold water and drain.

- In a small bowl mix together the soy sauce or fish sauce, ½ teaspoon salt, the brown sugar, cornstarch, and chile paste. Stir to dissolve the sugar and salt. Set aside.

- Season the chicken with salt. Heat a 14-inch flat-bottom wok or 12-inch steel skillet over high heat until a drop of water evaporates within a second or two when added to the pan. Swirl in 1 tablespoon of the oil by adding it to the sides of the pan and swirling the pan, then add the chicken in one layer. Let stand for 30 seconds without stirring, then stir-fry until cooked through, 3 to 5 minutes. Transfer to a bowl.

- Add the remaining oil and the garlic and ginger to the wok, and stir-fry for no more than 10 seconds. Add the peppers and stir-fry for 1 minute. Return the chicken along with any juices in the bowl to the wok. Add the zucchini noodles and soy sauce mixture, and stir together until the noodles are heated through and coated with the sauce. Add the cilantro, toss together quickly and remove from the heat. Serve with lime wedges.

ADVANCE PREPARATION This is all last-minute, though the vegetables can be prepped up to a day ahead and refrigerated.

Chicken Fajitas with
Spiralized Zucchini and Peppers

Makes 4 servings

½ pound zucchini

1 large red or yellow onion

2 red bell peppers

¼ cup fresh lime juice

Finely grated zest of 1 lime (about 1 teaspoon)

Salt

2 teaspoons cumin seeds, lightly toasted and ground

3 tablespoons adobo sauce from canned chipotles in adobo

6 tablespoons extra virgin olive oil, or ¼ cup olive oil plus 2 tablespoons grapeseed or canola oil

4 large garlic cloves, minced or put through a press

1½ pounds boneless, skinless chicken breast

Freshly ground black pepper

1 jalapeño or 2 serrano chiles, minced

¼ cup chopped cilantro

8 flour or corn tortillas

1 romaine heart, sliced crosswise

Red and/or green salsa

Queso fresco

I put as much emphasis on the vegetables as I do on the meat with my fajitas. I use the spiralizer to prepare the zucchini, peppers, and the onion, sear them in oil, then deglaze the pan with some of the marinade mixture. The idea of using the adobo sauce from canned chipotles in the marinade comes from cookbook author and host of Pati's Mexican Kitchen, *Pati Jinich. The same marinade works well with shrimp, though I like the shrimp equally well without the ancho sauce.*

SPIRALIZING THE ZUCCHINI Use the chipper (coarse shredder) blade. Take up handfuls of the spiralized zucchini and cut long strands into 2- to 3-inch lengths.

SPIRALIZING THE ONION Use the shredder blade. Insert the core (root end) of the onion into the cylinder.

SPIRALIZING THE PEPPERS Use the chipper (coarse shredder) blade. Insert the bottom end into the spiralizer tube and spiralize until you reach the seed pod. When you reach the seed pod, remove pepper from the spiralizer and cut the remaining flesh (about one-third of the pepper) away from the seed pod. Slice crosswise, the same thickness as the spiralized portion. Take up handfuls of the spiralized pepper and cut long strands into 2- to 3-inch lengths.

• In a small bowl or measuring cup combine the lime juice and zest, ¾ teaspoon salt, 1 teaspoon of the ground cumin, the adobo sauce, ¼ cup olive oil, and half the garlic. Mix well. Set aside 2 tablespoons.

• Season the chicken with salt and pepper, and place in a resealable bag. Pour in the marinade and seal bag. Move the chicken around to coat well, place the bag in a bowl, and refrigerate for 30 minutes to 12 hours. Massage the bag occasionally to redistribute marinade.

• Heat 2 tablespoons olive, grapeseed, or canola oil over medium-high in a large heavy skillet. When the oil is hot, add the onion and cook, stirring, until it softens and begins to color, 3 to 4 minutes. Stir in the peppers and chile, and cook, stirring, until the peppers begin to soften, about

continued on page 128

continued from page 126

3 minutes. Add the spiralized zucchini, the remaining garlic and cumin, and salt to taste, and cook, stirring often, until the vegetables are nicely seared, softened, and beginning to caramelize, about 8 minutes. Stir in the 2 tablespoons reserved marinade and cook, scraping the bottom of the pan to deglaze, for another 20 seconds to 1 minute. Taste and adjust seasoning. Stir in half the cilantro. Keep warm.

● Wrap the tortillas in foil and warm in the oven, or wrap in a towel and warm in a steamer or in the microwave.

● Heat the remaining oil over medium-high heat in a large heavy skillet. Remove the chicken breasts from the marinade, reserving the marinade, and pat dry. Add to the pan, rounded side down, and sear for 3 to 4 minutes, until lightly charred. Flip the breasts over, pour in the marinade, cover the pan and reduce the heat to medium. Cook 12 to 15 minutes, flipping the breasts over from time to time, until a thermometer registers 160 to 165 degrees when inserted into the thickest part. Transfer to a cutting board and cover with foil. Let stand 5 to 10 minutes.

● Arrange lettuce on a platter. Cut the chicken across the grain into ½- to ¾-inch-thick strips, and transfer to the platter next to lettuce. Tip the juices from the cutting board over the chicken and sprinkle with cilantro. Serve the vegetables on the same platter or on a separate platter with warm tortillas, salsa, and crumbled queso fresco.

VARIATION **Shrimp Fajitas**

● Substitute 1½ to 2 pounds large or medium shrimp for the chicken. Peel the shrimp. The adobo sauce can be omitted from the marinade. Marinate for 30 minutes only.

● Cook the shrimp in 2 tablespoons oil just until they begin to turn pink. Add marinade and continue to cook, stirring, until cooked through, another 2 to 3 minutes. Remove the shrimp from pan and reduce sauce, stirring, by half. Pour over the shrimp and serve.

VARIATION **Beef Fajitas**

The same vegetable mix can be used. Substitute the following rub and marinade for the chipotle marinade:

1 tablespoon cumin seeds, lightly toasted and ground

1 teaspoon chipotle or ancho chile powder

1 teaspoon salt

1¼ pounds flank steak

¼ cup fresh lime juice

   Finely grated zest of 1 lime (about 1 teaspoon)

¼ cup extra virgin olive oil

1 tablespoon Worcestershire sauce

4 large garlic cloves, minced

● Combine 2 teaspoons of the ground cumin, the chipotle or ancho chile powder, and 1 teaspoon salt. With a sharp knife, make shallow crosshatch cuts across the top and bottom surfaces of the steak. Rub the spice mix all over the surface of the steak (I recommend you wear gloves for this as the chile powder is hot). Place the steak in a resealable freezer bag.

● In a small bowl or measuring cup, whisk together the lime juice and zest, ¼ cup olive oil, the Worcestershire sauce, and half the garlic. Set aside 2 tablespoons of the marinade, and pour the rest into the bag with the steak. Seal and move the steak around in the bag to coat thoroughly. Place on a sheet pan and refrigerate. Marinate for 4 to 24 hours. Massage the bag occasionally to redistribute the marinade. Refrigerate the marinade you set aside if cooking the next day.

● Heat the tortillas and cook vegetables as directed in chicken recipe, using the remaining garlic and cumin and adding the marinade you set aside at the end of cooking to deglaze the pan and season the vegetables.

● To cook the meat, heat a large cast-iron skillet over medium-high heat, or prepare a medium-hot grill. Remove the meat from the marinade and discard marinade. Pat the meat dry with paper towels. If using a skillet, heat the remaining oil in the skillet and cook 3 to 4 minutes per side (if grilling, no need for the last tablespoon of oil). It should be medium rare. Remove to a cutting board, cover with foil, and let stand for 10 minutes, then cut across the grain into ½- to ¾-inch-wide strips. Proceed with the chicken fajita instructions for serving.

Rainbow Beef

Makes 4 generous servings

2 red bell peppers

1 orange or yellow bell pepper

1 green bell pepper

1 medium onion, peeled

1 pound lean flank steak

1½ teaspoons cornstarch

1 tablespoon plus 1 teaspoon rice wine or dry sherry

1 teaspoon soy sauce

2 fat garlic cloves, minced
Salt and freshly ground black pepper

1 teaspoon sesame oil

2 tablespoons hoisin sauce

2 tablespoons peanut oil, rice bran oil, or canola oil

1 tablespoon minced ginger

½ teaspoon red pepper flakes

1 Anaheim pepper, cut into 2-inch strips, or 1 jalapeño (for a spicier stir-fry), finely chopped
Spiralized uncooked daikon noodles or cooked spiralized turnip noodles or rice

This colorful mix of beef strips and an array of peppers and onion stir-fried with ginger, garlic, soy sauce, and hoisin is a classic. I use the spiralizer for the onion and peppers, and the prep—which is the only time-consuming part of stir-frying—goes quickly.

SPIRALIZING THE PEPPERS Use the chipper (coarse shredder) blade. Insert the bottom end into the spiralizer tube and spiralize until you reach the seed pod. When you reach the seed pod, remove pepper from the spiralizer and cut the remaining flesh (about one-third of the pepper) away from the seed pod. Slice crosswise, the same thickness as the spiralized portion. Take up handfuls of the spiralized peppers and cut long strands into 2-inch lengths with scissors.

SPIRALIZING THE ONION Use the shredder blade. Take up handfuls of the spiralized onion and cut long strands into 2-inch lengths with scissors.

● Slice the steak first with the grain into 2-inch-wide strips. Then cut each strip across the grain into ¼-inch thick slices. Place in a medium bowl and toss with the cornstarch, 1 teaspoon of the rice wine or sherry, the soy sauce, one of the minced garlic cloves, salt and pepper to taste, 1 teaspoon cold water, and the sesame oil.

● Combine the remaining rice wine or sherry and the hoisin sauce in a small bowl and set aside.

● Heat a 14-inch flat-bottom wok over high heat until a drop of water evaporates within a second or two when added to the pan. Swirl in 1 tablespoon of the peanut oil, and add the beef in a single layer. Let sit in the pan for about 1 minute, until it begins to sear, then stir-fry for 1 minute. Transfer to a plate or bowl.

● Swirl in the remaining peanut oil, then add the garlic, the ginger, and red pepper flakes and stir-fry for no more than 10 seconds. Add the onions and peppers, sprinkle with salt to taste, and stir-fry for 1 to 2 minutes. Return the beef and any juices that have accumulated on the plate or bowl to the wok; add the hoisin sauce mixture and stir-fry for another 30 seconds to a minute, until the beef is cooked through. Remove from the heat and serve with spiralized noodles or rice.

ADVANCE PREPARATION You can prep all ingredients a few hours ahead, but the stir-fry is a last-minute dish.

Chicken Tacos with Creamy Kohlrabi Slaw

Makes 4 servings

FOR THE CHICKEN

Finely grated zest from 1 lime (about 1 teaspoon)

3 tablespoons fresh lime juice
    Salt

1 teaspoon cumin seeds, lightly toasted and ground

1 to 2 chipotles in adobo, seeded and minced (to taste)

¼ cup extra virgin olive oil, or 3 tablespoons olive oil plus 1 tablespoon grapeseed or canola oil

2 large garlic cloves, minced or put through a press

1¼ to 1⅓ pounds boneless, skinless chicken breast
    Freshly ground black pepper

FOR THE SLAW

1 pound kohlrabi, peeled

4 to 6 fat radishes

¼ cup mayonnaise

¼ cup plain yogurt, the thicker the better (Greek is good)
    Salt

2 tablespoons seasoned rice vinegar

2 tablespoons fresh lime juice
    Finely grated zest from 1 lime (about 1 teaspoon)

3 tablespoons chopped cilantro

8 corn tortillas
    Quick Tomatillo Salsa (page 135, optional)

I have always had a weakness for creamy coleslaw. This one has a particularly satisfying texture, with a little bite from the radishes. The chicken gets a kick from its chipotle-lime marinade. The coleslaw will throw off a fair amount of juice, which you can leave behind in the bowl when you top the tacos. The slaw will still be creamy.

SPIRALIZING THE KOHLRABI
Peel the kohlrabi twice to be sure that you have gotten rid of the tough outer skin. Use the shredder blade.

SPIRALIZING THE RADISHES
Use the shredder blade.

● In a small bowl or measuring cup combine the lime zest and juice, ¾ teaspoon salt, the ground cumin, chipotles, 3 tablespoons of the olive oil, and the garlic. Mix well.

● Season the chicken with salt and pepper, and place in a resealable bag. Pour in the marinade and seal the bag. Move the chicken around to coat well; place the bag in a bowl and marinate for 30 minutes to 12 hours. If marinating for longer than 30 minutes, refrigerate. Flip the bag over from time to time to redistribute the marinade.

● Meanwhile, make the coleslaw. Spiralize the kohlrabi and the radishes. Whisk together the mayonnaise, yogurt, salt to taste, rice vinegar, lime juice, and lime zest. Stir in the cilantro. Toss with the kohlrabi and radishes. Refrigerate until ready to use.

● Heat 1 tablespoon olive, grapeseed, or canola oil over medium-high heat in a large heavy skillet. Remove the chicken breasts from the marinade, reserving the marinade; pat dry and sear on the rounded side for 3 to 4 minutes, until lightly charred. Flip the breasts over, pour in the marinade, cover the pan, and reduce the heat to medium. Cook 12 to 15 minutes, depending on the thickness of the

continued on page 134

continued from page 133

chicken breasts, until cooked through and a meat thermometer registers 160 degrees when tested in the thickest part. Remove from the heat, let stand for 5 to 10 minutes, then slice across the grain, about ⅓ inch thick. Pull the pieces apart into two or three pieces.

• Warm the tortillas and arrange the chicken on top. Spoon on a little salsa if desired, and top with coleslaw.

VARIATION **Po'boys with Chicken and Coleslaw**

• Substitute 4 soft buns or hot dog buns for the tortillas. Arrange a small amount of coleslaw on the bottom half of each bun, top with chicken, and top with more coleslaw and the top bun.

Quick Tomatillo Salsa

Makes 2 cups, serving 6 to 8

1 pound tomatillos, husked and rinsed

2 jalapeño or serrano chiles, seeded for a milder salsa, coarsely chopped

¼ cup chopped onion, soaked for 5 minutes in cold water, drained, and rinsed

1 garlic clove, peeled

¼ to ½ cup coarsely chopped cilantro

¼ to ½ cup water, as needed

Salt

Tomatillo salsas are tangy and spicy. They go well with potatoes and greens, eggs and zucchini, chicken and seafood of all kinds. This one is very quick to throw together. The tomatillos require either a quick roast or a simmer, then everything is blended, and it's done!

● Either simmer the tomatillos in water to cover for 8 to 10 minutes, flipping them over halfway through, until softened and olive green, or roast under the broiler. To do this, preheat the broiler, cover a baking sheet with foil, and place the tomatillos on top, stem side down. Place under the broiler at the highest rack setting, and broil 2 to 5 minutes, until charred on one side. Turn over and broil on the other side for 2 to 5 minutes, until charred on the other side. Remove from the heat. Transfer to a blender, tipping in any juices that may have accumulated on the foil. Add the chiles, onion, garlic, cilantro, and ¼ cup water to the blender; blend to a coarse puree. Transfer to a bowl, add salt to taste (about ½ teaspoon), and thin out as desired with water. Taste and adjust salt, and chill for at least 30 minutes before serving, to allow the flavors to develop. Thin out if desired with more water (it will thicken in the refrigerator).

ADVANCE PREPARATION This will hold for 3 or 4 days in the refrigerator, but the fresher it is, the more vivid the flavors will be.

Tacos with Winter Squash and Chipotles

Makes 4 servings

2 pounds butternut squash with long necks

3 tablespoons extra virgin olive oil

Salt

2 to 4 chipotle chiles in adobo, minced

1 tablespoon adobo sauce from chiles

4 ounces queso blanco or feta, crumbled (1 cup)

8 corn tortillas

Winter squash and chipotles make a wonderful pairing—the sweetness of the winter squash is set off by the heat of the chiles, and vice versa. The texture and flavor of the roasted squash strips is particularly satisfying.

SPIRALIZING THE SQUASH Peel the entire squash, making sure to peel off the tough outer layer just underneath the skin. Trim the ends. Cut the neck of the squash away from the bulbous bottom. Spiralize the neck with the chipper (coarse shredder) blade. Take up handfuls of the spiralized squash and cut long strands into 2- to 3-inch lengths with scissors.

● Preheat the oven to 400 degrees. Line 2 baking sheets with parchment. Spiralize the neck of the squash as directed and place in a large bowl. Peel and seed the bottom bulbous part, and cut in ½-inch dice. Place the spiralized squash on one baking sheet and the diced squash on the other. Toss the spiralized portion with 2 tablespoons of the olive oil and salt to taste, and the diced portion with 1 tablespoon oil and salt to taste. Place in the oven and roast for 20 to 30 minutes, stirring every 10 minutes (tongs work well for this), or until tender and caramelized, switching the pans top to bottom halfway through. Remove from the oven and transfer the squash from both baking sheets to a bowl.

● Add the chipotles, adobo sauce, and half the cheese to the squash and stir together.

● Heat the tortillas. Fill the bottom of a steamer with ½ inch of water and bring to a boil. Meanwhile, wrap the tortillas in a heavy kitchen towel and place in the steamer basket above the boiling water. Cover tightly and steam 1 minute, then turn off the heat but do not uncover. Let stand for 10 minutes. Alternatively, wrap in a towel and heat in the microwave 1 to 2 minutes.

● Place two hot tortillas on each plate, and top each one with the squash. Sprinkle queso fresco over the top and fold the tacos over.

ADVANCE PREPARATION The cooked squash will keep for a few days in the refrigerator. Transfer to a lightly oiled baking dish and reheat in a low oven.

Tacos with Potatoes, Onions, and Greens

Makes 4 servings

1½ pounds red boiling potatoes, Yukon golds, or russets, peeled if desired and trimmed

1 medium or large red or white onion

6 cups tightly packed Swiss chard leaves, or other greens such as kale, beet greens, watermelon radish greens, or mustard greens (about ½ pound)

Salt

3 tablespoons extra virgin olive oil

Freshly ground black pepper

2 garlic cloves, minced

½ teaspoon dried oregano, preferably Mexican

8 corn tortillas

Quick Tomatillo Salsa (page 135)

2 ounces Mexican queso fresco or feta, crumbled (½ cup)

An abundance of vegetables is packed into these comforting tacos. You can use whatever greens you like. I've used Swiss chard, kale, beet greens, and watermelon radish greens. They all work well.

SPIRALIZING THE POTATOES Use the chipper (coarse shredder) blade. Take up handfuls of the spiralized potato and cut long strands into 2-inch lengths with scissors.

SPIRALIZING THE ONION Use the shredder blade. If necessary, take up handfuls of the spiralized onion and cut long strands into manageable lengths with scissors.

● Bring a pot of water to a boil while you wash and stem the greens. When the water comes to a boil, salt generously and add the greens. Blanch for 1 to 3 minutes depending on the green (kale takes longest), until just tender. Transfer to a bowl of cold water and drain. Take up by the handful and squeeze out excess water. Chop coarsely and set aside.

● Heat 1 tablespoon of the olive oil over medium heat in a large heavy skillet. Add the onion and cook, stirring, until lightly browned, 5 to 10 minutes. If the onion begins to stick and brown too much before it becomes tender, add a generous pinch of salt. Remove from the pan and transfer to a bowl. Add the remaining 2 tablespoons oil to the pan and when hot, add the potatoes. Season with salt and pepper and cook, stirring often, until tender, 10 to 15 minutes. Add the garlic and oregano, and stir for 1 minute, until fragrant. Stir the onion back into the pan along with the greens. Stir together and season generously with salt and pepper.

● Spoon onto hot tortillas, top with green salsa, and sprinkle with cheese, if using. Serve with additional salsa.

ADVANCE PREPARATION You can make the filling up to a day ahead. Reheat in a skillet on the stove.

Tacos with Summer Squash and Eggs

Makes 4 servings

¾ pound zucchini or yellow summer squash, or a mix

1 tablespoon extra virgin olive oil

1 or 2 garlic cloves (to taste), minced

Salt and freshly ground black pepper

6 to 8 eggs

2 tablespoons milk

2 tablespoons minced fresh chives

8 corn tortillas, warmed

Crumbled queso fresco or feta

Salsa

I love tacos filled with eggs and vegetables of all kinds, whether I'm eating them for dinner or for breakfast. This mix of zucchini and eggs is particularly appealing. I used to grate the zucchini; now I spiralize it on the shredder blade and cut the strands into shorter lengths with scissors.

SPIRALIZING THE SQUASH Use the shredder blade. Take up handfuls of the spiralized squash and cut long strands into 2- to 3-inch lengths with scissors.

● Heat the olive oil over medium-high heat in a large heavy pan and add the spiralized squash. Cook, stirring often, until it wilts, about 3 minutes. Add the garlic and continue to cook, stirring, for another 1 to 2 minutes, until the mixture is very fragrant. Season to taste with salt and pepper. Turn the heat down to medium.

● Beat the eggs in a medium bowl. Add the milk and salt and pepper to taste, and whisk together. Stir in the chives. Add to the pan with the squash and cook, stirring every few seconds with a wooden spoon or a rubber spatula, until the eggs are set with large curds. Remove from the heat.

● Fill warm corn tortillas with the zucchini and eggs, sprinkle with queso fresco or feta, and serve with salsa on the side.

ADVANCE PREPARATION The vegetable filling can be prepared through Step 1 several hours before scrambling the eggs. Reheat until the zucchini is sizzling, and proceed with the recipe.

Side Dishes

I had so much fun putting together this chapter. Who can complain when the fruit of a day's recipe testing is homemade potato chips, shoestring fries, or crispy, feathery latkes made with unexpected ingredients like beets and herbs, or sweet potatoes and chipotles?

Spiralized vegetables, with their even, flat surfaces, definitely lend themselves to crisp-frying in hot oil. The slicer blade is a perfect tool for cutting very thin rounds that can be fried for chips, and the coarse blade is much easier and safer to use than a mandoline for cutting thin strips for shoestring fries. I also like to make onion fritters with clumps of thin spiralized onions dipped in batter (page156).

Other side dishes that I make often and quickly with the help of my spiralizer are the savory Mediterranean pepper stew on page 167 and the watermelon Radishes with Greens and Gremolata on page 160. During the month of August, when there is more squash than I know what to do with at my farmers market and a bounty of sweet summer corn, I make succotash (page 164) weekly. Prep goes quickly when I use the spiralizer.

You can also serve spiralized noodles as a side dish. Count on a little less per person than I suggest in the pasta chapter—maybe 4 to 6 ounces rather than 8 ounces. Toss winter squash and sweet potato noodles with a couple of tablespoons of olive oil, and roast in the oven on a parchment-covered baking sheet (see instructions for winter squash in the recipe for Winter Squash Noodles with Miso-Glazed Salmon and Leeks, page 120. Cook other noodles in salted boiling water, toss with a little olive oil or butter, and, if you wish, a little Peanut Dukkah (page 156) or Parmesan, and enjoy.

Curly Shoestring Fries

Makes 3 to 4 servings

2 large russet potatoes (about 1 pound 10 ounces), peeled if desired

Canola, peanut, or grapeseed oil for frying

Salt

The spiralizer is much easier to use than a mandoline for cutting potatoes into thin strips for shoestring fries. Although russet potatoes are the best for these because they are so high in starch, I have also made them successfully with Yukon golds, which are slightly less starchy. You will still get shoestrings that are browned and crispy on the edges and nice and soft inside.

SPIRALIZING THE POTATOES Use the chipper (coarse shredder) blade. Take up handfuls of the spiralized potatoes and cut into 2- to 3-inch lengths with scissors.

• Pour oil to a depth of at least 2 inches into a wok or a heavy wide saucepan or Dutch oven (or heat oil in a deep fryer). Heat oil over medium heat until it reaches 375 degrees on a deep-fry thermometer.

• Meanwhile, rinse the spiralized potatoes well under cold water. Drain well on kitchen towels and pat dry. The dryer they are, the better they will crisp. Divide into four batches.

• Place a rack over a baking sheet and place near the pot with the oil. When the oil reaches 375 degrees, working in batches, add potatoes to the oil and stir constantly with a skimmer or slotted spoon. Maintain the oil temperature at 350 degrees. Fry until the potatoes are light brown and crisp, about 3 minutes. Using a skimmer or slotted spoon, transfer from the oil to the rack, holding the skimmer over the oil briefly to allow the oil to drip back into pot. Allow the oil to come back up to temperature between batches.

• Sprinkle with salt while still hot.

VARIATION **Shoestring Sweet Potato Fries**

• Substitute sweet potatoes for the potatoes.

Potato Chips

Makes 3 to 4 servings

2 large russet potatoes (about
  1 pound 10 ounces), or the
  equivalent amount of Yukon
  golds, peeled if desired
  Canola, peanut, or grapeseed
  oil for frying
  Salt

The spiralizer is the perfect tool for making your own potato chips, which will be better than anything you will ever find in a bag. The slicer blade makes thin, wide spirals that you can easily cut into rounds and deep-fry to a perfect crisp.

● Follow the recipe for Curly Shoestring Fries (page 144), but use the slicer blade to cut the potatoes. Cut the spiralized potatoes into rounds. You can also achieve rounds by making a ½-inch incision down one side of the potato.

ADVANCE PREPARATION These will remain crisp for a few hours. Put them in a brown bag and take them to the movies!

Sweet Potato Chipotle Latkes

Makes about 30 small latkes, serving 6

2 pounds red-flesh sweet
   potatoes (yams), peeled if
   desired, ends trimmed

2 good-size chipotle chiles in
   adobo, seeded and minced

2 tablespoons adobo sauce
   from chipotles

2 teaspoons ground cumin
   Salt

¼ cup almond meal

2 tablespoons cornstarch

2 eggs, beaten
   Canola, grapeseed, or rice
   bran oil for frying

2 teaspoons finely grated
   lime zest

1 cup thick plain yogurt or
   Greek yogurt, crème fraîche,
   or sour cream

Latkes made with spiralized vegetables are lacy and crisp. They are particularly pretty, and because they are thin, they are lighter than traditional latkes. Chipotles packed in adobo sauce, which are hot but also sweet and pungent, go beautifully with red-flesh sweet potatoes here.

SPIRALIZING THE SWEET POTATOES Use the shredder blade. Take up handfuls of the spiralized sweet potatoes and cut long strands into 2- to 3-inch lengths with scissors.

• Place the spiralized sweet potatoes in a large bowl. Toss with the chipotle chiles and adobo sauce, cumin, salt to taste, the almond meal, and cornstarch. Add the beaten eggs and stir together.

• Preheat the oven to 300 degrees. Place a rack over a baking sheet.

• Heat ¼ inch of oil in a large skillet over medium-high heat until rippling. Drop the latke mixture by heaped tablespoons into the oil, then flatten at once with the back of the tablespoon or with a spatula. The spiralized strands should fan out a bit in the pan. Cook for 2 to 3 minutes, until nicely browned. Slide a spatula or tongs underneath and flip the latkes over. Cook on the other side until golden brown, another 2 to 3 minutes. Adjust heat down if the latkes burn, but keep the oil hot enough so they crisp nicely. Transfer to the rack set over a baking sheet, and place in the oven to keep warm. Continue until all of the latkes are cooked.

• Stir the lime zest into the yogurt, crème fraîche, or sour cream. Spoon on top of the latkes or serve on the side.

ADVANCE PREPARATION You can prep the ingredients and combine everything except the eggs and salt several hours ahead. Refrigerate in a large bowl. Don't add salt until you're ready to cook, or the mixture will become watery, as salt draws the water out of the vegetables.

Spicy Carrot, Parsnip, and Potato Latkes

Makes about 3 dozen, serving 8

1 pound mixed carrots and parsnips, peeled and trimmed

1¼ to 1½ pounds russet potatoes, peeled if desired and trimmed

1 teaspoon baking powder

Salt and freshly ground black pepper

2 serrano chiles or 1 jalapeño, minced (seeded if desired)

½ cup chopped cilantro

1 tablespoon nigella seeds

¼ cup chopped chives

¼ cup cornstarch

2 eggs, beaten

Canola, grapeseed, or rice bran oil for frying

Plain Greek yogurt, crème fraîche, chutney, or sour cream (optional)

You can use whatever proportion of carrots to parsnips you prefer. Because parsnips are easier to spiralize, I tend to use more of them than carrots, but any proportion works. The vegetable mixture is spicy, with chiles contributing heat, and depth of flavor coming from nigella seeds and cilantro.

SPIRALIZING THE CARROTS AND PARSNIPS Use the shredder blade. Take up handfuls of the spiralized carrots and parsnips and cut long strands into 2- to 3-inch lengths with scissors.

SPIRALIZING THE POTATOES Use the shredder blade. Take up handfuls and cut long strands into 2- to 3-inch lengths with scissors.

• Preheat the oven to 300 degrees. Place a rack over a baking sheet.

• In a large bowl mix together the spiralized carrots, parsnips, and potatoes, the baking powder, salt and pepper to taste, the chiles, cilantro, nigella seeds, chives, and cornstarch. Add the eggs and stir together.

• Heat a large heavy skillet over medium-high heat. Add ¼ inch of oil, and when it is rippling hot, take up heaped tablespoons or small handfuls of the latke mixture, press the mixture against the spoon to extract liquid (or squeeze in your hands), and place in the pan. Press down with a spatula to flatten. The spiralized strands should fan out a bit in the pan. Repeat with more spoonfuls, being careful not to crowd the pan. Cook on one side until golden brown, about 3 minutes. Slide a spatula or tongs underneath and flip the latkes over. Cook on the other side until golden brown, another 2 to 3 minutes. Transfer to the rack set over a baking sheet and place in the oven to keep warm.

• Serve hot topped with Greek yogurt, crème fraîche, or sour cream, or other toppings of your choice such as salsa, chutney, or yogurt blended with cilantro, mint, and garlic.

ADVANCE PREPARATION It's best to make these as soon as you prep the ingredients so the potatoes don't discolor.

Potato and Kale Latkes

Makes 2 to 2½ dozen, serving 6

2 large russet potatoes (about
1½ pounds), peeled and
trimmed

1 bunch scallions or spring
onions, white and light green
parts only, minced

½ pound kale, stemmed, washed,
dried, and finely chopped or
cut into thin slivers (about
3 cups tightly packed)

2 teaspoons cumin seeds, lightly
toasted and coarsely ground

1 teaspoon baking powder
Salt and freshly ground black
pepper

2 tablespoons minced chives

¼ cup cornstarch

2 eggs, beaten
Canola, grapeseed, or rice
bran oil for frying
Thick yogurt, sour cream,
crème fraîche, or Cucumber
and Watermelon Radish Raita
(page163)

Another irresistible latke made with spiralized potatoes, which fan out in the pan and become crispy on the edges. They are mixed with finely chopped kale and seasoned with cumin. I like to serve these with raita.

SPIRALIZING THE POTATOES Use the shredder blade. Take up handfuls and cut long strands of the spiralized potatoes into 2-inch lengths with scissors.

• Preheat the oven to 300 degrees. Place a rack over a baking sheet.

• In a large bowl mix together the spiralized potatoes, the scallions or spring onions, kale, cumin, baking powder, salt and pepper to taste, chives, and cornstarch. Add the eggs and stir together.

• Heat about ¼ inch of oil in a wide heavy skillet over medium-high heat. When it is hot, take up heaped tablespoons of the latke mixture, press the mixture against the spoon to extract liquid (or squeeze in your hands), and place in the pan. Press down with the back of the spatula to flatten. The spiralized strands of potato should fan out a bit in the pan. Repeat with more spoonfuls, being careful not to crowd the pan. Turn heat to medium. Cook on one side until golden brown, about 3 minutes. Slide the spatula underneath and flip the latkes over. Cook on the other side until golden brown, another 2 to 3 minutes. Transfer to the rack set over a baking sheet, and place in the oven to keep warm. The mixture will continue to release liquid, which will accumulate in the bottom of the bowl. Stir from time to time, and remember to squeeze the heaped tablespoons of the mix before you add them to the pan.

• Serve hot topped with yogurt, crème fraîche, or sour cream, or other toppings of your choice such as salsa, chutney, or raita.

ADVANCE PREPARATION It's best to make these as soon as you prep the ingredients so the potatoes don't discolor.

Beet and Herb Latkes

Makes about 30 latkes, serving 6

1 to 1¼ pounds beets
(4 medium)

1 pound russet potatoes
(2 medium), peeled and
trimmed

Salt

2 eggs

½ cup chopped mixed fresh
herbs such as dill, mint, parsley,
cilantro

2 teaspoons cumin seeds, lightly
toasted and ground

1 teaspoon ground caraway

¼ cup cornstarch

Freshly ground black pepper

¼ cup grapeseed or canola oil
(more as needed)

Plain Greek yogurt, crème
fraîche, or sour cream

These colorful, crisp latkes made with spiralized beets and potatoes mixed with an abundance of fresh herbs taste of North Africa, seasoned as they are with cumin and caraway.

SPIRALIZING THE BEETS Use the shredder blade. Take up handfuls of spiralized beets and cut long strands into 2-inch lengths with scissors.

SPIRALIZING THE POTATOES Use the shredder blade. Take up handfuls of the spiralized potatoes and cut long strands into 2-inch lengths with scissors.

• Salt the spiralized beets generously and leave to drain in a colander for 30 minutes, tossing and squeezing the beets from time to time (wear rubber gloves to protect your hands from the color). Take up the spiralized beets by the handful, squeeze out as much water as you can, and transfer to a bowl.

• In a large bowl beat the eggs and add the beets, the spiralized potatoes, the herbs, cumin, caraway, cornstarch, ½ teaspoon salt (or more to taste), and pepper to taste. Mix together well.

• Preheat the oven to 300 degrees. Place a rack over a baking sheet.

• Heat about ¼ inch oil in a large heavy skillet over medium-high heat. When it is hot, take up heaped tablespoons of the latke mixture, press the mixture against the spoon to extract liquid (or squeeze in your hands), and place in the pan. Press down with the back of a spatula to flatten. Repeat with more spoonfuls, being careful not to crowd the pan. The spiralized beets and potatoes should fan out a bit in the pan. Cook on one side until golden brown, about 3 minutes. Slide the spatula or tongs underneath and flip the latkes over. Cook on the other side until golden brown, another 2 to 3 minutes. Transfer to the rack set over a baking sheet, and place in the oven to keep warm. The mixture will continue to release liquid, which will accumulate in the bottom of the bowl. Stir from time to time, and remember to squeeze the heaped tablespoons of the mix before you add them to the pan.

• Serve with yogurt, crème fraîche, or sour cream.

ADVANCE PREPARATION You can salt and drain the beets several hours ahead. It's best to make these as soon as you prep the remaining ingredients so the potatoes don't discolor.

Onion Fritters with Middle Eastern Spice Mix

Makes 4 to 6 servings

1 pound red or yellow onions

¾ cup plus 2 tablespoons cornstarch

7 tablespoons corn flour or very fine cornmeal

¾ teaspoon salt

¾ teaspoon ground cumin

1 cup cold sparkling water

⅓ cup finely chopped cilantro

3 tablespoons Peanut Dukkah (recipe below)

Canola oil or grapeseed oil for frying

The spiralizer makes a quick job of slicing onions. And no tears! Take them up by the handful and dip the clump into this seasoned gluten-free tempura batter, then deep-fry them, and you've got something way better than onion rings. Make sure the clumps are small. If you try to dip and fry too thick a handful, it won't crisp up properly.

SPIRALIZING THE ONION Use the chipper (coarse shredder) blade.

- Place the spiralized onions in a bowl and cover with cold water. Let stand 5 minutes. Drain, rinse, and drain well on paper towels.

- In a medium bowl whisk together the cornstarch, corn flour, salt, and cumin. Whisk in the sparkling water. Stir in the cilantro and dukkah.

- Pour oil to a depth of 3 inches into a wok or wide saucepan and heat over medium-high heat to 375 degrees. Place a rack on a baking sheet, and set it next to the wok. Have a spider strainer or deep-fry skimmer handy for removing the fritters from the oil.

- Take up a small clump of onions and dip into the batter, making sure to coat thoroughly. Carefully transfer to the hot oil and deep-fry until golden brown, which should take only a minute or two. Flip over with the spider strainer to make sure the coating is evenly fried. It's important not to crowd pan and to let the oil come back up to temperature between batches.

- Using a skimmer, strainer, or tongs, remove the fritters from the oil, allowing excess oil to drip back into the wok, and drain on the rack. Sprinkle with salt right away if desired. Allow to cool slightly and serve right away.

PEANUT DUKKAH Chop ½ cup lightly toasted unsalted peanuts very fine. Mix with ¼ cup lightly toasted sesame seeds in a bowl. In a dry skillet lightly toast 2 tablespoons coriander seeds just until fragrant, and immediately transfer to a spice mill and allow to cool. In the same skillet toast 1 tablespoon cumin seeds just until fragrant, and transfer to the spice mill. When the spices have cooled, grind and add to the nuts and sesame seeds. Add 2 teaspoons nigella seeds, 1 teaspoon ground sumac, and ½ teaspoon kosher salt or coarse sea salt, and mix together. Makes about ⅔ cup.

ADVANCE PREPARATION Keep dukkah in a jar in the refrigerator for up to a month.

Vegetable Spring Rolls with Tofu

Makes 8 spring rolls

½ recipe Southeast Asian Carrot and Daikon Radish Slaw (page 34)

2 tablespoons Peanut-Ginger Sauce (recipe below) or soy sauce

¼ pound firm tofu, cut into ¼-inch thick by ½-inch wide dominoes and drained on paper towels

8 8½-inch rice flour spring roll wrappers

16 sprigs cilantro

Leaves from several sprigs fresh mint

Leaves from several sprigs Thai basil (may substitute regular basil if you can't get the Thai variety) or tarragon

8 to 10 inner romaine lettuce leaves, cut in chiffonade (crosswise strips)

NOTE If the wrapper tears when you roll it, you can moisten another wrapper and roll the torn one in that one. Two wrappers will not make an overly thick roll.

Vegetable spring rolls are as easy to make as burritos—easier really. I fill the delicate rice flour wrappers with tofu and Southeast Asian Carrot and Daikon Radish Slaw.

● Prepare slaw for filling. Spread a small amount of Peanut-Ginger Sauce onto each cut piece of tofu, or toss with soy sauce.

● Fill a bowl with warm water, and place a spring roll wrapper in it just until pliable, about 30 seconds. Remove from the water and drain briefly on a kitchen towel. Place the wrapper on your work surface, and arrange several cilantro sprigs, whole mint leaves, and basil or tarragon leaves, vein side up, on the wrapper. Leaving a 2-inch margin on the sides, place a handful of the slaw on the wrapper, slightly nearer to the edge closest to you. Top with three pieces of tofu, then a handful of lettuce. Fold in the sides, then roll up the spring rolls tightly, squeezing the filling to get a tight roll. Refrigerate until ready to serve. If desired, serve with more Peanut-Ginger Sauce, thinned out with water, or with another dipping sauce of your choice.

PEANUT-GINGER SAUCE In a small bowl whisk together 3 tablespoons creamy unsalted, unsweetened peanut butter, 1 tablespoon rice vinegar, 2 teaspoons soy sauce, 1 to 2 teaspoons light brown sugar to taste, 1½ teaspoons ginger juice (grate 1 tablespoon ginger, wrap in cheesecloth, and squeeze), and cayenne to taste. Spread onto the tofu pieces. For serving, add 2 to 4 tablespoons water or more as desired to thin out

ADVANCE PREPARATION These will keep for a day in the refrigerator.

Watermelon Radishes with Greens and Gremolata

Makes 2 servings

6 watermelon radishes, with greens attached, or use 1 generous bunch mustard greens or turnip greens if radishes come without greens attached

Salt

2 tablespoons extra virgin olive oil

1 large garlic clove, minced

2 teaspoons fresh thyme leaves

Freshly ground black pepper

1 tablespoon Gremolata (recipe below)

2 eggs, fried or poached (optional)

Crumbled feta (optional)

Watermelon radishes resemble turnips in their appearance. Like turnips, they can be cooked. A brief sauté is all they need. You can serve this as a side dish or as a more substantial main dish topped with an egg. If you don't buy the watermelon radishes with the greens attached, substitute mustard greens or turnip greens.

SPIRALIZING THE WATERMELON RADISHES Cut the radishes away from the greens, peel and trim the ends flat. Use the shredder blade. Cut the inner core into thin slices.

• Bring a large pot of water to a boil and salt generously. Fill a bowl with cold water. Strip the greens from the tough stems. Discard the stems. Wash the leaves in two changes of water. A generous bunch (1¼ to 1½ pounds) should give you 7 to 8 cups greens.

• Blanch the greens for 2 to 3 minutes, until just tender to the bite. Transfer to the bowl of cold water, then drain and squeeze out excess water by taking up handfuls and squeezing hard. Cut each fistful into strips ¼ to ½ inch wide.

• Heat the oil over medium heat in a large heavy skillet. Add the garlic and thyme, and cook, stirring, until the garlic is fragrant, 30 seconds to a minute. Stir in the spiralized radishes and cook, stirring, for 1 minute. Add the greens, stir together, and season with salt and pepper. Cook, stirring, for another minute. Stir in the gremolata. Remove from the heat.

• Top each serving with a fried or poached egg and/or a sprinkling of feta, if desired.

GREMOLATA Toss together 1 to 2 garlic cloves, finely minced; ¼ cup finely minced flat-leaf parsley; and 2 teaspoons finely chopped lemon zest.

ADVANCE PREPARATION The cooked greens will keep for 3 to 4 days in the refrigerator.

Cucumber and
Watermelon Radish Raita

Makes 2 cups, serving 4 to 6

1 European cucumber or 1 large regular cucumber (12 to 14 ounces), peeled if desired

Salt

3 watermelon radishes, peeled

1½ cups plain yogurt (not fat-free)

1 teaspoon cumin seeds, lightly toasted and ground

½ teaspoon coriander seeds, lightly toasted and ground

2 to 3 tablespoons finely chopped cilantro, to taste

1 to 2 serrano or bird chiles, finely chopped (optional)

Raita is a mix of yogurt, spices and/or herbs, and often vegetables. It makes a cooling accompaniment to curries and can stand alone as a salad. It's terrific with all of the latkes in this collection.

SPIRALIZING THE CUCUMBER Use the chipper (coarse shredder) blade. Take up handfuls of the spiralized cucumber and cut long strands into bite-size lengths with scissors.

SPIRALIZING THE WATERMELON RADISHES Use the chipper (coarse shredder) blade. Take up handfuls of the spiralized radishes and cut long strands into bite-size lengths with scissors.

● Place the spiralized cucumber in a colander and sprinkle with salt. Let sit in the sink for 15 to 30 minutes, then rinse briefly and drain on paper towels.

● Place the cucumber and radishes in a bowl. Add the remaining ingredients and stir together. Season to taste with salt. Refrigerate until ready to serve.

ADVANCE PREPARATION This will keep for a couple of days in the refrigerator. You will have to stir it as the cucumbers will release water into the mixture.

Succotash with Black Beans

Makes 6 servings

1 red onion, peeled

1½ pounds mixed zucchini and yellow summer squash

1 red bell pepper

2 tablespoons extra virgin olive oil

2 plump garlic cloves, minced
Kernels from 2 ears of corn
Salt

1 teaspoon fresh thyme leaves

1 (15-ounce) can black beans, drained and rinsed
Freshly ground black pepper

3 to 4 tablespoons chopped cilantro or parsley

½ cup (2 ounces) crumbled feta cheese (optional)

When I was a kid, I hated lima beans; it was the texture that didn't appeal to me. So later in life, even though I had come to enjoy lima beans, I developed a recipe for a succotash with black beans standing in for the limas. The spiralizer reduces prep time considerably, and the dish is beautiful to behold.

SPIRALIZING THE RED ONION Use the shredder blade.

SPIRALIZING THE SUMMER SQUASH Use the chipper (coarse shredder) blade. Take up handfuls and cut long strands of the spiralized squash into 2-inch lengths with scissors, or make a ½-inch incision down the length of the squash to get half moons.

SPIRALIZING THE RED PEPPER Use the chipper (coarse shredder) blade. Insert the bottom end into the spiralizer tube and spiralize until you reach the seed pod. When you reach the seed pod, remove from the spiralizer and cut the remaining flesh (about one-third of the pepper) away from the seed pod. Slice crosswise the same thickness as the spiralized portion. Take up handfuls of the spiralized red pepper and cut long strands into 2-inch lengths with scissors.

- Heat the olive oil in a large heavy skillet over medium heat, and add the spiralized onion. Cook, stirring often, until tender, 5 to 8 minutes, and add the garlic, spiralized summer squash, spiralized red pepper, corn kernels, about ¾ teaspoon salt, and the thyme leaves. Turn the heat to medium-high and cook, stirring, until the squash is translucent and the corn and red pepper are tender, 10 to 15 minutes.

- Stir in the black beans and heat through. Add freshly ground pepper, taste, and adjust salt. Stir in the cilantro or parsley, and remove from the heat. Top with feta if desired. Serve as a side dish, or use as a filling for tacos.

ADVANCE PREPARATION The succotash will keep for 2 to 3 days in the refrigerator.

Spiralized Pepper Stew

Makes 4 to 6 servings

2 large red bell peppers (or 1 red and 1 yellow pepper)

1 large green bell pepper

2 tablespoons extra virgin olive oil

1 medium onion, peeled and chopped

2 garlic cloves, minced

1 Anaheim pepper, cut into 2- to 3-inch strips (optional)

Salt

1 (14-ounce) can chopped tomatoes, drained of some but not all of its juice

⅛ teaspoon sugar

Freshly ground black pepper

I serve this colorful pepper stew as a side dish, but I also use it as a filling for frittatas and omelets, an accompaniment to pasta, and as the base for risotto. You can also stir eggs into it and scramble them for pipérade (page 82).

SPIRALIZING THE PEPPERS Use the chipper (coarse shredder) blade. Insert the bottom end of the pepper into the spiralizer tube and spiralize until you reach the seedpod. Remove the portion with the seedpod (approximately one-third of the pepper), cut away the pepper from the pod, and cut the pieces crosswise the same width as the spiralized pepper. Take up handfuls of the spiralized pepper and cut long strands into 2- to 3-inch lengths with scissors.

● Heat the oil over medium heat in a large heavy skillet or casserole, and add the onion. Cook, stirring, until tender, about 5 minutes, and add the garlic, all of the spiralized peppers, the Anaheim pepper, and salt to taste. Cook, stirring often, until the peppers are tender, about 8 minutes.

● Add the tomatoes, sugar, salt, and black pepper to taste. Bring to a simmer and simmer until the tomatoes have cooked down somewhat, stirring from time to time; simmer about 10 minutes. Cover, reduce the heat, and simmer another 10 to 15 minutes, until the mixture is thick and fragrant. Taste and adjust seasoning.

ADVANCE PREPARATION The stewed peppers will keep for about 5 days in the refrigerator.

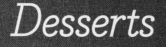

Desserts

You can make enticing and beautiful fruit-based desserts with the help of the spiralizer. While most fruit is too soft to spiralize (or has pits), apples, pears, and Asian pears are ideal. The tool simultaneously cores and cuts these fruits into slices or curved strips.

I use the fruit in crumbles and soufflés, parfaits and cakes, rice pudding and pancakes. You'll also find deconstructed baked apples and pears, the fruit arranged in ramekins, the top layer beautifully spiraled, glazed at the end of baking, and topped with ice cream or custard sauce.

The spiralizer is an excellent tool to use when you want ultra-thin slices, as you do with the Pear Upside-Down Cake on page 185, in which paper-thin pears are layered over a mix of brown sugar and melted butter and topped with a pound cake batter.

When you spiralize apples and pears, the strands may break apart. This is a factor of their width and texture. Since I cut up most of the fruit with scissors after spiralizing, this won't really be an issue for most of these desserts; even for the ramekins, you can piece the curved sections together for the top layer. Make sure to have lemon juice or lime juice ready when you spiralize so you can toss the fruit with the juice right away to prevent it from discoloring.

Coconut Black Rice Pudding with Asian Pear and Blueberries

Makes 6 servings

1 large Asian pear, peeled

½ cup black rice

1 cup water

¼ teaspoon salt

1 cup milk or rice beverage

1 cup unsweetened low-fat coconut milk

¼ cup mild honey or agave syrup

1 teaspoon vanilla extract

1 cup blueberries

This heavenly dessert (or breakfast) is an adaptation of a recipe by pastry chef Sherry Yard. I spiralize a sweet-tart Asian pear, cut it into small pieces, and stir it with blueberries into the black rice, which turns purple when cooked. If you use a rice beverage and agave syrup, it makes an outstanding vegan rice pudding. It's very important to use low-fat coconut milk; the fat from full-fat coconut milk can congeal on top of the pudding when you chill it.

SPIRALIZING THE ASIAN PEAR Use the chipper (coarse shredder) blade. Take up handfuls of the spiralized pear and cut long strands into bite-size lengths with scissors.

● Combine the rice, water, and salt in a saucepan, and bring to a boil. Reduce the heat, cover, and simmer 35 to 40 minutes, until all of the water is absorbed.

● Add the milk, coconut milk, and honey to the rice and stir together. Bring to a boil, stirring. Reduce the heat and simmer, stirring often, for about 15 minutes, or until creamy (the mixture will continue to thicken when you chill it). Add the vanilla, the spiralized Asian pear, and the blueberries, and continue to simmer for another 5 minutes.

● Scrape into a bowl or individual serving dishes. Cover and chill for at least 2 hours before serving.

ADVANCE PREPARATION You can make this a day or two ahead and keep in a covered bowl in the refrigerator.

Blueberry, Pear, and Yogurt Parfait

Makes 4 servings

1 ripe but firm pear, peeled

2 tablespoons lime juice

⅓ cup sugar

¼ to ½ teaspoon fresh ginger juice (see Note)

2¼ cups blueberries

½ teaspoon balsamic vinegar

2 tablespoons crème de cassis liqueur

½ teaspoon cornstarch dissolved in 1 tablespoon water (optional)

3 cups plain or vanilla Greek yogurt

1 tablespoon finely chopped shelled pistachios

NOTE To make the ginger juice, finely chop 2 to 3 tablespoons fresh ginger. Wrap in a piece of cheesecloth. Hold the cheesecloth over a bowl and twist and squeeze to extract the juice.

Serve these handsome parfaits as dessert or breakfast. The juicy layer of spiralized pear, spiced with fresh ginger, is a hidden surprise in the middle. The blueberries can seem watery when you simmer them, but the mixture thickens as it cools. I've given the option of thickening the mixture with a light cornstarch slurry if you think it isn't thickening quickly enough.

SPIRALIZING THE PEAR Use the chipper (coarse shredder) blade. Take up handfuls of the spiralized pear and cut long strands into 2-inch lengths with scissors.

● Toss the spiralized pears with 1 tablespoon of the lime juice, 1 tablespoon of the sugar, and the ginger juice.

● Combine the blueberries, remaining sugar and lime juice, balsamic vinegar, and crème de cassis in a medium saucepan, and bring to a boil over medium heat. Cook for 10 to 15 minutes, until the liquid is reduced and the blueberries have cooked down to a jamlike consistency. If the mixture seems very watery, add the cornstarch (if using) and stir until the liquid thickens (it will thicken without the cornstarch as the mixture cools). Allow to cool. You should have about 1 cup of thick sauce.

● Spoon ¼ cup yogurt into each of four tumblers or parfait glasses. Top with a tablespoon of the blueberry sauce. Make another ¼-cup layer of yogurt, and top with a layer of spiralized pear. Add another layer of yogurt and top with a layer of blueberry sauce. Cover tightly and chill for at least 1 hour. Just before serving, sprinkle finely chopped pistachios over the top.

ADVANCE PREPARATION The assembled parfaits will hold in the refrigerator for a day. Sprinkle on the pistachios just before serving.

Blueberry-Apple Pancakes

Makes 12 4-inch pancakes

1 large or 2 small crisp, tart apples, such as a Braeburn or Granny Smith, peeled

1 tablespoon butter, plus butter for the griddle

2 teaspoons brown sugar

1 cup whole wheat flour

½ cup unbleached all-purpose flour (or ½ cup whole wheat flour)

2 teaspoons baking powder

1 teaspoon baking soda

1 tablespoon sugar

¼ teaspoon salt

2 large eggs

1½ cups buttermilk

1 teaspoon vanilla extract

3 tablespoons canola oil

1 cup fresh or frozen blueberries

Butter and maple syrup for serving

Before my son went off to boarding school, I kept a constant supply of blueberry pancakes in the freezer for quick weekday pancake breakfasts. With the spiralizer I added another dimension to my buttermilk pancake formula. I spiralize apples (pears will also work), caramelize them a little bit in butter, and add a small handful to each pancake. My son noticed them right away when he was last home from school, and gave me a thumbs up on this new pancake.

SPIRALIZING THE APPLE Use the chipper (coarse shredder) blade. Take up handfuls and cut long strands of the spiralized apple into 2-inch lengths with scissors

• Heat the 1 tablespoon butter in a large nonstick pan over high heat. When the foam subsides, add the spiralized apples and the brown sugar. Sauté for about 3 minutes, just until beginning to color. Remove from the heat.

• Preheat a griddle. Sift together the flours, baking powder, baking soda, sugar, and salt.

• In another bowl whisk the eggs, then add the buttermilk and whisk together. Whisk in the vanilla and oil.

• Add the flour mixture to the wet ingredients, and quickly whisk together. Do not overbeat; a few lumps are okay.

• Brush the griddle with butter. Drop batter by half-ladles or ¼-cup ladles (3 to 4 tablespoons) onto the hot griddle. Place a clump of apples and six or seven blueberries on each pancake. Cook until bubbles begin to break through, 2 to 3 minutes. Turn and cook for about 1 minute on the other side, or until nicely browned. Remove from the heat and continue until all of the batter is used.

• Serve hot with butter and maple syrup.

ADVANCE PREPARATION The pancakes freeze well. I freeze them in stacks of three or four, wrapped tightly in plastic, then bagged in a freezer bag.

Apple Soufflé

Makes 6 servings

5 good-size Granny Smith apples (about 2½ pounds), peeled
Juice of 1 lemon
½ cup plus 2 tablespoons sugar
1 teaspoon vanilla extract
¼ teaspoon powdered ginger
Butter for the soufflé dish or ramekins
8 large egg whites
⅛ teaspoon cream of tartar

Dessert soufflés are easy to make and always impressive. Most of the apples here are cooked down into an applesauce that is folded into an egg white and sugar meringue. But I hold back one apple for the spiralizer, and that uncooked apple adds wonderful texture and a lively tart fresh fruit element to the airy soufflé.

SPIRALIZING THE APPLES Set aside one of the apples. Use the chipper (coarse shredder) blade for the other four apples. Cut long strands into 2-inch lengths with scissors. Toss with half the lemon juice. After you have made the applesauce, spiralize the remaining apple on the shredder blade. Cut long strands into 2-inch lengths with scissors.

• Place the four spiralized apples in a large heavy saucepan. Add 2 tablespoons of the sugar, the vanilla, ginger, and 2 tablespoons water, and bring to a simmer over medium heat. Stir, turn the heat down to low, cover, and simmer, stirring often, for 20 minutes. Uncover and continue to simmer for another 20 to 25 minutes, stirring often, until the fruit has cooked down to a slightly chunky applesauce and is beginning to stick to the pan. Transfer to a large bowl and allow to cool.

• Preheat the oven to 425 degrees with the rack adjusted to the lowest position. Butter one 2-quart soufflé dish or six 6-ounce ramekins, and dust with sugar (use about 1½ tablespoons of the sugar).

• Toss the remaining spiralized apple with 2 tablespoons sugar and 1 tablespoon lemon juice.

• In the bowl of a standing mixer fitted with the whisk attachment, or in a large bowl with a hand mixer, beat the egg whites on low speed for 1 minute, or until they foam. Add the cream of tartar and continue to beat on low speed for 1 minute. Turn the speed to medium, and slowly stream in the remaining sugar while you continue to beat to firm, satiny peaks. Be careful not to overbeat.

• Fold one-third of the egg whites into the applesauce to lighten it. Fold in the rest, along with the spiralized apple. Gently spoon into the ramekins or the soufflé dish, mounding it up over the top.

• Place the ramekins or soufflé dish on a baking sheet, and place in the oven. Bake individual soufflés for 10 to 15 minutes, until puffed and golden. They should still be runny on the inside. Bake a large soufflé for 15 minutes, then turn the heat down to 375 degrees. Continue to bake for another 10 minutes, until puffed and the top is dark golden brown. Serve at once.

Baked Spiralized Apple Ramekins with Vanilla Ice Cream

Makes 6 servings

1½ pounds apples, such as Granny Smith or Braeburn, peeled

2 tablespoons fresh lemon juice

2 tablespoons butter, plus additional for the ramekins

4 tablespoons raw brown or organic white sugar

1½ teaspoons cinnamon

½ teaspoon freshly grated nutmeg

½ teaspoon allspice

2 tablespoons apricot jam

Vanilla ice cream

This is a beautiful dessert, a sort of deconstructed baked apple topped with a scoop of vanilla ice cream. When I was developing the dessert, I spent a lot of time layering perfect spirals of apple. Finally it occurred to me that only the top layer needed to look like a spiral. So if your apple comes out of the spiralizer broken into shorter pieces, which happens more often than not, no worries, you'll only need enough neat spirals for the top layers of each ramekin, and you can piece them together from the broken bits.

SPIRALIZING THE APPLES Use the chipper (coarse shredder) blade. Toss with the lemon juice.

• Preheat the oven to 350 degrees. Generously butter six 4-inch, shallow crème brulée ramekins.

• In a small bowl combine the sugar, cinnamon, nutmeg, and allspice.

• Make a layer of spiralized apple in a ramekin. This can be either a neat spiral that covers the bottom of the dish, or a thin layer of broken-up spiralized apple. Sprinkle with the sugar mix and dot with butter. Repeat with 2 or 3 more layers. The top layer should be a neat spiral. Dot with butter and sprinkle with sugar mix. Repeat with remaining ramekins.

• Place all of the ramekins on a sheet pan and bake 30 to 35 minutes, until bubbling and soft when pierced with a knife.

• Heat the apricot jam in a small saucepan until melted enough to brush onto the tops of the apples. Glaze the top of each apple ramekin with jam.

• Just before serving, place a scoop of vanilla ice cream in the center of each ramekin.

ADVANCE PREPARATION The ramekins can be baked several hours before serving. Reheat in a low oven to serve warm.

VARIATION Substitute coconut oil for the butter.

Baked Spiralized Pear Ramekins with Custard Sauce

Makes 6 servings

FOR THE CUSTARD SAUCE

1¼ cups milk

½ vanilla bean, split and scraped

¼ teaspoon powdered ginger

2 egg yolks

¼ cup sugar

FOR THE PEARS

1½ pounds pears, peeled

2 tablespoons fresh lemon juice

2 tablespoons butter, plus additional for the ramekins

4 tablespoons raw brown or organic white sugar

1½ teaspoons cinnamon

½ teaspoon ground ginger

This is much like the baked spiralized apples on page 178, but instead of serving the pears with ice cream, I make a vanilla custard sauce (crème anglaise) to spoon over the warm ramekins. You could substitute ice cream though. I also use ginger in the sugar/spice mix because I love the way pears and ginger go together.

SPIRALIZING THE PEARS Use the chipper (coarse shredder) blade. Toss with the lemon juice.

TO MAKE THE CUSTARD SAUCE

• Set aside ¼ cup of the milk. Place the remaining 1 cup milk in a saucepan. Using the tip of a paring knife, split the vanilla bean down the middle and scrape the seeds into the milk. Place the pods in the milk, add the powdered ginger, and bring to a boil. As soon as the milk reaches a boil, turn off the heat, cover the pan tightly with plastic, and let stand for 20 minutes. Remove the vanilla bean pods from the milk and scrape again so all of the seeds go into the milk. Set the pods aside (rinse them, allow them to dry out completely for a day or two, and stick them into a jar of sugar).

• Fill a large bowl with ice cubes, and place a medium bowl on top of the ice cubes with a strainer set over the bowl.

• In another bowl combine the egg yolks and half the sugar, and beat together for about 30 seconds. Beat in the ¼ cup milk you set aside.

• Add the remaining sugar to the milk in the saucepan, and bring back to a simmer while stirring with a heatproof rubber spatula. When the sugar has dissolved, turn off the heat. Place your bowl with the beaten egg yolks next to the saucepan, with a towel coiled around the bottom to keep it steady, and whisk in two-thirds of the hot milk. Whisk the egg-milk mixture back into the saucepan with the remaining milk.

• Place the saucepan back on low heat. Using a rubber spatula, stir constantly and everywhere until you feel the mixture starting to thicken. Stirring in a figure 8 helps to assure that your spatula touches the entire bottom of the pan. Place a thermometer in the saucepan and continue to stir constantly until the temperature reaches between 165 degrees and

180 degrees. Lift your spatula from the saucepan with some sauce on it and run your finger down the middle. It should leave a canal.

- Immediately strain the mixture into the clean dry mixing bowl set in the ice. Stir for a few minutes, then once in a while, until the mixture has cooled to 40 degrees F. The mixture should cool down in 20 minutes or less. If you do not have enough ice on hand, place the bowl in your freezer and stir once in a while. Once cool, transfer to a container, cover tightly, and refrigerate until ready to use.

TO PREPARE AND BAKE THE PEARS

- Preheat the oven to 350 degrees. Generously butter six 4-inch, shallow crème brulée ramekins.

- In a small bowl, combine the sugar, cinnamon, and ginger.

- Make a layer of spiralized pear in a ramekin. This can be either a neat spiral that covers the bottom of the dish, or a thin layer of broken-up spiralized pear. Sprinkle with the sugar mix and dot with butter. Repeat with 2 or 3 more layers. The top layer should be a neat spiral. Dot with butter and sprinkle with sugar mix. Repeat with remaining ramekins.

- Place all of the ramekins on a baking sheet and bake 30 to 35 minutes, until bubbling and soft when pierced with a knife.

- Spoon the custard sauce over the pears to serve.

ADVANCE PREPARATION The ramekins can be baked several hours before serving. Reheat in a low oven to serve warm.

Pear Crisp with Pecan Topping

Makes 6 to 8 servings

FOR THE TOPPING

1¼ cups rolled oats

½ cup whole wheat pastry flour, millet flour, or quinoa flour

2 teaspoons finely chopped or grated orange zest

⅓ cup unrefined turbinado sugar

¼ teaspoon salt

½ teaspoon freshly grated nutmeg

3 ounces (6 tablespoons) cold unsalted butter, cut into ½-inch pieces

⅓ cup coarsely chopped pecans

FOR THE PEAR FILLING

2½ to 3 pounds pears (about 5 large), peeled

Butter

2 tablespoons raw brown (turbinado) sugar, preferably organic

1 tablespoon fresh lemon juice

2 tablespoons chopped candied ginger

1 teaspoon vanilla extract

2 teaspoons cornstarch or arrowroot

I have always had a weakness for crumbles and crisps. The spiralizer speeds up prep for this one, slicing the pears paper thin and coring them at the same time. The topping works equally well with a gluten-free flour like millet or quinoa as it does with regular whole wheat.

SPIRALIZING THE PEARS Cut a ½-inch deep slice down one side of the pear and use the slicer blade.

• Make the crisp topping first. Preheat the oven to 350 degrees. Cover a baking sheet with parchment. Place the oats, flour, orange zest, sugar, salt, and nutmeg in a food processor fitted with the steel blade and pulse several times to combine. Add the butter and pulse until the butter is evenly distributed throughout the grain mix. Add the pecans and pulse briefly to combine. The mixture should have a crumbly consistency. You can also mix this together in a stand mixer fitted with the paddle.

• Spread the topping over the parchment-covered baking sheet in an even layer. Bake 10 minutes. Rotate the pan front to back, stir the mixture, and bake another 5 to 10 minutes, until nicely browned. Remove from the heat and allow to cool.

• To make the crisp, preheat the oven to 375 degrees. Butter a 2-quart baking dish. In a large bowl mix together the pears, sugar, lemon juice, candied ginger, vanilla, and cornstarch or arrowroot.

• Scrape the fruit and all of the juice in the bowl into the baking dish. Set the baking dish on a baking sheet to facilitate handling, and place in the oven. Bake 20 to 25 minutes, until the fruit is bubbling and the liquid is syrupy. Remove from the oven and allow to cool, if desired.

• About 30 minutes before serving, spread the crisp topping over the pear mixture in an even layer. Bake 15 to 20 minutes, or until the fruit is bubbling and the topping is nicely browned. Remove from the heat and allow to cool for at least 10 minutes before serving.

ADVANCE PREPARATION The topping keeps for several weeks in the freezer in an airtight container or freezer bag. The crisp can be baked through Step 4 several hours ahead.

Pear Upside-Down Cake

Makes 10 servings

FOR THE TOPPING

- 3 ripe but firm pears (about 1 pound 2 ounces), peeled
- Juice of 1 small lime
- 85 grams / 3 ounces / ¾ stick unsalted butter (6 tablespoons)
- 150 grams / 1 cup tightly packed light brown sugar
- 1 tablespoon dark rum

FOR THE CAKE

- 185 grams / approximately 1½ cups all-purpose flour
- 1½ teaspoons baking powder
- ½ teaspoon salt
- 115 grams / 4 ounces / 1 stick butter (½ cup)
- 200 grams / approximately 1 cup sugar
- 150 grams / 3 large eggs
- 1 teaspoon vanilla extract
- 1 teaspoon dark rum
- 125 grams / ½ cup milk

For this classic upside-down cake, I slice the pears on the spiralizer and layer the thin slices onto a mix of brown sugar and butter. It's a rich, comforting cake that never fails to please a crowd. Anjou pears, which taper more evenly than other varieties, are good for the spiralizer. I'm giving measures here in grams and cups because I find that pastry making is more precise when you use grams.

SPIRALIZING THE PEARS Use the slicer blade. Toss the thinly sliced pears with the lime juice and set aside.

- Before you begin, bring all of your ingredients to room temperature.

- Preheat the oven to 350 degrees. Butter a 9-inch round cake pan and line the bottom with parchment. Butter the parchment.

- For the topping, in a small saucepan over medium heat, combine the butter and brown sugar, and heat until the butter and the brown sugar have melted together. Stir in the rum. Transfer to the cake pan and spread in an even layer using a small offset spatula.

- Drain the pears and fan out in even, thin layers over the butter mixture.

- For the cake, sift together the flour, baking powder, and salt. Set aside.

- In the bowl of a stand mixer fitted with the paddle attachment, beat the butter on medium speed for 2 minutes, until fluffy. Scrape down the bowl and beaters, and add the sugar. Cream for another 2 minutes on medium speed, until light and fluffy. Scrape down the bowl and beaters. Add the eggs, one at a time, scraping down the bowl and beaters after each addition. Add the vanilla extract and the rum, and beat together.

- On low speed, add the milk and the flour mixture, alternating wet and dry ingredients.

- Pour the batter over the pears, and gently smooth with an offset spatula. Place the pan on a baking sheet, and bake for 50 minutes, or until golden brown and a tester comes out clean. Set the pan on a rack, and allow the cake to rest for 15 minutes in the pan. The top of the cake tends to rise over the edges of the pan and settle, which is fine. Run a knife between the cake overlap and the pan, flip onto a serving platter, and allow to cool or serve warm.

ADVANCE PREPARATION The cake keeps for a few days. Cover and keep at room temperature or refrigerate.

Index